I0372038

# MAJESTY AND MERCY

God Through the Eyes of Isaiah : 2022 Berean Study Series

Edited by
**BILL BAGENTS**

Majesty and Mercy: God Through the Eyes of Isaiah

Published by Heritage Christian University

Copyright © 2022 by Bill Bagents

Manufactured in the United States of America

Cataloging-in-Publication Data

Majesty and mercy: God through the eyes of Isaiah / edited by Bill Bagents

p. cm.

Includes scripture index.

ISBN 978-1-956811-06-3 (pbk.) 978-1-956811-07-0 (ebook)

1. Bible. Isaiah—Study and Teaching I. Bagents, William Ronald, 1956–, editor. II. Title.

224.1007—dc20

Library of Congress Control Number: 2021924184

Cover design by Brad McKinnon and Brittany Vander Maas.
All rights reserved. No part of this publication may be reproduced, distributed, stored in a retrieval system, or transmitted in any form or by any means without the prior written permission of the publisher, except in the case of brief quotations embodied in critical reviews and certain other noncommercial uses permitted by copyright law.
For information:
Heritage Christian University Press
3625 Helton Drive
PO Box HCU
Florence, AL 35630

www.hcu.edu

# CONTENTS

| | |
|---|---:|
| Bible Abbreviations | v |
| Introduction | ix |
| 1. THE MOUNTAIN OF THE LORD'S HOUSE<br>C. Wayne Kilpatrick | 1 |
| 2. A VISION OF HOLINESS<br>W. Kirk Brothers | 12 |
| 3. THE COMING KING<br>Ed Gallagher | 20 |
| 4. YHWH IS OUR GOD<br>Tim Martin | 34 |
| 5. GOD'S PEACE<br>Thomas Tidwell | 43 |
| 6. CORNERSTONE AND CROWN OF GLORY<br>Will Dilbeck | 52 |
| 7. THE REIGN OF RIGHTEOUSNESS<br>Michael Jackson | 61 |
| 8. THE HIGHWAY OF HOLINESS<br>Keith Stanglin | 69 |
| 9. GOD'S COMFORT<br>Bill Bagents | 79 |
| 10. BEAUTIFUL FEET<br>Todd Johnston | 87 |
| 11. THE SUFFERING SERVANT<br>Justin Guin | 97 |

12. GOD'S HIGHER WAY — 107
Ismael Berlanga

13. GOD'S ANOINTED — 115
Jeremy Barrier

Scripture Index — 123
Contributors — 131
Credits — 135
Berean Study Series Titles — 137
Coming in 2023 — 139
Heritage Christian University Press — 141

# BIBLE ABBREVIATIONS

**Old Testament**

| | |
|---|---|
| Gen | Genesis |
| Exod | Exodus |
| Lev | Leviticus |
| Num | Numbers |
| Deut | Deuteronomy |
| Josh | Joshua |
| Judg | Judges |
| Ruth | Ruth |
| 1–2 Sam | 1–2 Samuel |
| 1–2 Kgs | 1–2 Kings |
| 1–2 Chr | 1–2 Chronicles |
| Ezra | Ezra |
| Neh | Nehemiah |
| Esth | Esther |
| Job | Job |
| Ps | Psalms |

| | |
|---|---|
| Prov | Proverbs |
| Eccl | Ecclesiastes |
| Song | Song of Solomon |
| Isa | Isaiah |
| Jer | Jeremiah |
| Lam | Lamentations |
| Ezek | Ezekiel |
| Dan | Daniel |
| Hos | Hosea |
| Joel | Joel |
| Amos | Amos |
| Obad | Obadiah |
| Jonah | Jonah |
| Mic | Micah |
| Nah | Nahum |
| Hab | Habakkuk |
| Zeph | Zephaniah |
| Hag | Haggai |
| Zech | Zechariah |
| Mal | Malachi |

## New Testament

| | |
|---|---|
| Matt | Matthew |
| Mark | Mark |
| Luke | Luke |
| John | John |
| Acts | Acts |
| Rom | Romans |
| 1–2 Cor | 1–2 Corinthians |

| | |
|---|---|
| Gal | Galatians |
| Eph | Ephesians |
| Phil | Philippians |
| Col | Colossians |
| 1–2 Thess | 1–2 Thessalonians |
| 1–2 Tim | 1–2 Timothy |
| Titus | Titus |
| Phlm | Philemon |
| Heb | Hebrews |
| Jas | James |
| 1–2 Pet | 1–2 Peter |
| 1–2–3 John | 1–2–3 John |
| Jude | Jude |
| Rev | Revelation |

# INTRODUCTION

When the first Gospel writer told the story of Jesus, he started with Isaiah: "As it is written in the prophet Isaiah ..." (Mark 1:2).[1] The New Testament quotes the book of Isaiah some 65 further times, making it the second most quoted Old Testament book in the New Testament (after Psalms). Early Christians found the oracles of Isaiah to be profoundly meaningful as they reflected on their experience of Jesus, and they saw God's ancient promises coming to fulfillment in their midst. Isaiah continued to play a leading role in the church's theological writings.[2] In the late fourth century, Jerome translated Isaiah from Hebrew into Latin, prefixing to his translation a brief preface, in which he wrote: Isaiah

> should be called not so much a prophet as an evangelist. For he clearly pursues all the mysteries of Christ

and of the Church, so that you would not think he was predicting the future but composing a history about the past.[3]

Isaiah is a difficult book, a fact recognized by early Christians, as well. In that same preface to Isaiah, Jerome also acknowledged, "Nor am I ignorant how much work it takes to understand the Prophets," and Isaiah specifically. A few years before Jerome wrote those words, Augustine, the future bishop of Hippo and theological giant in western Christian history, wanted to begin reading the Bible after becoming enamored with the preaching of Ambrose of Milan. He asked Ambrose for advice, as he later recalled in his *Confessions*, addressed to God.

> I asked him to advise me concerning the best way to go about reading your Scriptures, so that I could be better prepared and fitter to receive such great grace. He recommended the prophet Isaiah, I think because he foretells, more clearly than anyone else, the Gospel and the calling of the Gentiles. But when I began to read it, I could make no sense of it; and thinking the whole book would be more of the same, I decided to put off any further reading until I had become better acquainted with the Lord's way of speaking.[4]

Augustine's experience is surely not unique, which

makes me wonder at Ambrose's advice. Despite its importance in the New Testament and in Christian history, Isaiah is not the book I'd recommend to someone beginning a study of Scripture. It can be confusing, both in its overall structure and in its individual sentences. And so it is often neglected in the church today.

But let me say this for Ambrose: his instincts were correct—if you want to progress in your understanding of God and his dealings with humans, you've got to spend time with Isaiah. This volume of the Berean Study Series aims to make your time with Isaiah a little easier and more profitable.

## HISTORICAL BACKGROUND

The book of Isaiah explains in the very first verse the historical time period of the prophet. (This is often the case with the prophets: if you want to know when they lived, turn to the first verse.)

> The vision of Isaiah son of Amoz, which he saw concerning Judah and Jerusalem in the days of Uzziah, Jotham, Ahaz, and Hezekiah, kings of Judah. (Isa 1:1)

The fact that only "kings of Judah" are named in this verse already helps us to locate Isaiah in the South, the kingdom of Judah, rather than the North, the kingdom of Israel. Most of the prophets who have books named after them also prophesied in the South. The four kings named as contemporary with Isaiah reigned during the second half of the eighth century BC, so our time period for Isaiah is roughly 740–700 BC. The earliest, dated oracle/vision in the book is at Isaiah 6, dated to the year that King Uzziah died. There is some disagreement on the exact chronology of events in ancient Israel, but I think it's safe to say that Uzziah died sometime around 740 BC. The last dated event in the book is the invasion of Judah by the Assyrians, led by King Sennacherib, which took place in 701 BC (see Isa 36–37).

Isaiah lived while Assyria was the dominant empire in the Near East, which would remain true long after his lifetime. Assyria's capital, Nineveh, was sacked in 612 BC, a date that usefully marks the transition from the domination of Assyria to the domination of Babylon. It was Babylon, led by Nebuchadnezzar, that God used to take Judah captive for a couple generations (see 2 Kgs 24–25; Jer 25). Some of the prophecies in the book of Isaiah also deal with this time period, the period of exile. Especially in Isaiah 40–48, the oracles concern the end of the exile.

> Go out from Babylon, flee from Chaldea,
> > declare this with a shout of joy, proclaim it,
> > send it forth to the end of the earth;
> > say, "The LORD has redeemed his servant Jacob!"
> (Isa 48:20)

This redemption was historically fulfilled when Babylon was itself overtaken by the Persians, led by Cyrus the Great, who announced that the Jews could return to their ancestral land (Ezra 1:1–4). The book of Isaiah even names Cyrus as God's agent of redemption (Isa 44:28; 45:1).

The horizon of the book of Isaiah is not exhausted even by these historical time periods, nor will it ever be exhausted, until we live in the new heavens and new earth imagined in the book (Isa 65:17). But as for what usually counts as historical background, we can keep in mind these dates.

Isaiah's ministry: 740–700 BC
Assyrian period: 745–612 BC
Babylonian period: 612–539 BC
Exile: 597 BC–539 BC
Destruction of Jerusalem temple: 586 BC
Persian period: 539–330 BC

## STRUCTURE

It will help to have a basic outline of the book of Isaiah in your head. The most basic outline divides the book into two major sections:

Isaiah 1–39
Isaiah 40–66

These two sections differ in several ways, which you can easily tell just by reading through the book. The first section has a few scattered headings (1:1; 2:1;

13:1), has stories about Isaiah and his interactions with kings (e.g., Isaiah 7; 36–39), has oracles about his contemporary situation in the Assyrian period. The second section has none of that, but is a 27-chapter collection of oracles about the end of the exile and life after the exile. Now, I've painted with a broad brush; the two sections are not as distinct as all that. There are some oracles in the first section that deal with issues that have little to do with Isaiah's own historical period, such as the destruction of Babylon (Isa 13–14). But the general distinction I have made will be helpful to keep in mind: up through chapter 39, the book deals often with Isaiah's own time period, whereas after that the book focuses on the end of the exile.

We can get more detailed, especially for the first section. There are some headings in the text that help us navigate the book (2:1; 13:1), so we can see that chapters 2–12 form a distinct unit, labeled "The word that Isaiah son of Amoz saw concerning Judah and Jerusalem" (2:1). The heading at 13:1 says that we're about to read an oracle against Babylon, and that oracle ends at 14:23, after which we immediately read an oracle against Assyria (14:24–27), and then one against the Philistines (14:29–32), and then Moab (chapters 15–16), and so. It is apparent that we have entered a section of Oracles against the Nations, a class of oracles common to all three major prophetic books (Isa 13–23; Jer 46–51; Ezek 25–32). Also easily spotted in this first major section of Isaiah are the prose stories about Isaiah and Hezekiah at the end of the section (chapters 36–39).

We can construct an outline for the first major section of Isaiah like this:

Chapter 1: Introduction

Chapters 2–12: Oracles about Judah and Jerusalem (reign of Ahaz)

Chapters 13–23: Oracles against the Nations

Chapters 24–27: Isaiah Apocalypse

Chapters 28–35: Oracles during the time of Hezekiah

Chapters 36–39: Stories about Isaiah and Hezekiah

## POETRY

One reason that Isaiah can be difficult is that it is written in poetry. It's not the only reason Isaiah is difficult; Paul managed to write some difficult letters (as Peter recognized! 2 Pet 3.16) without composing poetic lines. Old Testament prophetic oracles are often written in poetry, though, and much of Isaiah's book is poetic. (Same for Job, Psalms, Proverbs, Song of Songs.) But it is not poetry as we may be accustomed to thinking of poetry; it does not rhyme, nor does it have a strict meter or rhythm, either in English translation or in the original Hebrew.

For a long time readers of Isaiah did not realize that it was written in poetry.[5] In that preface to Isaiah by Jerome that I've already quoted a couple times, he explicitly says that the prophets are not written in poetry. The discovery of the nature of Hebrew poetry in the modern period is attributed to Robert Lowth, one time Professor of Poetry at Oxford and later Bishop of London. In 1741, he lectured on *The Sacred Poetry of the Hebrews*, and his book of lectures was published in 1753.[6]

I won't go into this subject very deeply, partly because I'm not a very good analyst of poetry.[7] Lowth's great insight was that Hebrew poetry made heavy use of parallel lines, where two lines echo one another in some way.

> Hear, O heavens, and listen, O earth;
> > for the LORD has spoken:
> > I reared children and brought them up,
> > but they have rebelled against me.
> > The ox knows its owner,
> > and the donkey it's master's crib;
> > but Israel does not know,
> > my people do not understand. (Isa 1:2–3)

This beginning of the oracles of Isaiah illustrates some of the issues. You can see the parallelism especially in verse 3: "The ox knows its owner, / and the donkey it's master's crib." Ox is parallel to donkey, and owner is parallel to master's crib. On the other hand, verse 2 doesn't have a parallelistic structure, at least not one that is as obvious as in verse 3. That's the way it is;

sometimes it's obvious, sometimes it's not. But when you have a passage with a bunch of parallel lines, you're probably reading poetry.

And like with a lot of poetry in different cultures, Hebrew poetry is generally harder to read than Hebrew prose. Poetry tends to use more imagery than prose, more figurative language, so it's a little more ambiguous. And poetry tends to use obscure words, sometimes archaic words, or sometimes it will simply leave words out that are usually there in prose. Your translation solves some of these problems for you: the English translators supply some of the missing words in order to make the text more readable, and even though the Hebrew words that are present in the text might be obscure and archaic, translators invariably translate those hard Hebrew words with easy English words. But there's a catch: the English translation is going to be easier than the Hebrew is—meaning, it might be wrong. A hard Hebrew word might be able to be translated in a few different ways, but an English translator has to pick one of those ways. That kind of thing is sometimes a problem when reading Hebrew prose, but it is often a problem when reading Hebrew poetry. The upshot is that it is a wise move, when you're really trying to study a passage, to compare different translations, and it is especially important to do so when studying a poetic text like Isaiah. Different translators will make different decisions on how to understand the passage, and comparing their results will give you a better idea of the different possibilities of the words of Isaiah.

## TEXT

In the winter of 1946/47, a teenage bedouin shepherd boy threw a rock in a cave in the Judean desert northwest of the Dead Sea and heard a crash. His investigation revealed several leather scrolls, including what came to be recognized as a complete copy of the book of Isaiah in Hebrew (and another copy, unfortunately not complete), dating to around the time of Jesus and therefore nearly a thousand years older than the previously known Hebrew copies of the book. This discovery of a few manuscripts was the first in a string of manuscript discoveries, the Dead Sea Scrolls, eventually totaling about 900 scrolls, of which more than 200 were copies of books of the Hebrew Bible. As it turned out, that first scroll of Isaiah, the Great Isaiah Scroll, was the only complete copy of a biblical book to be discovered among the Dead Sea Scrolls; all the other copies are fragmentary. The group that stored the scrolls in those caves near the Dead Sea was especially interested in Isaiah, since twenty-one copies of the book have been discovered, topped only by Psalms (36 copies) and Deuteronomy (30 copies).

The text of Isaiah in your English Bible is a translation from the Hebrew text of Isaiah; the same is true for the entire Old Testament. Since the Dead Sea

Scrolls provide us mostly with fragmentary copies of the biblical books, we have to rely on medieval Hebrew copies for a complete Hebrew Bible. The earliest complete copy of the Hebrew Bible is known as the Leningrad Codex and dates to about the year AD 1009. English translators start with this manuscript—again, because it is the earliest complete copy. But there are other sources for the text of Isaiah that sometimes help to correct the Leningrad Codex, under the assumption that the Leningrad Codex does not provide a perfect copy of the Hebrew Bible but contains some copyist mistakes. These other sources for the text of the Hebrew Bible include primarily the Dead Sea Scrolls and the Septuagint. The Septuagint (abbreviated LXX) is the Greek translation of the Old Testament originally produced in the centuries just before the time of Jesus. The Dead Sea Scrolls and the LXX provide much older evidence for the text of the Bible than the Leningrad Codex. Sometimes the notes in your Bible refer to these other sources of information.

## ISAIAH IN THE NEW TESTAMENT

I've already mentioned that Isaiah was hugely influential in the New Testament, that it was the second most quoted Old Testament book in the New Testament. To drive home the importance of the oracles of Isaiah for the proclamation of the Christian gospel, I conclude this introduction with a list of these quotations.

# PASSAGES OF ISAIAH QUOTED IN THE NEW TESTAMENT.

| 1:9 | Romans 9:29 |
|---|---|
| 6:9 | Luke 8:10 |
| 6:9–10 | Matthew 13:14–15 |
| | Mark 4:12 |
| 6:9–10 | Acts 28:26–27 |
| 6:10 | John 12:40 |
| 7:14 | Matthew 1:23 |
| 8:8, 10 | Matthew 1:23 |
| 8:14 | Romans 9:33 |
| | 1 Peter 2:8 |
| 8:17 | Hebrews 2:13 |
| 8:18 | Hebrews 2:13 |
| 9:1–2 | Matthew 4:15–16 |
| 10:22–23 | Romans 9:27–28 |
| 11:10 | Romans 15:12 |
| 22:13 | 1 Corinthians 15:32 |
| 25:8 | 1 Corinthians 15:54 |
| 27:9 | Romans 11:27b |
| 28:11–12 | 1 Corinthians 14:21 |
| 28:16 | Romans 9:33 |
| | Romans 10:11 |
| | 1 Peter 2:6 |
| 29:10 | Romans 11:8 |
| 29:13 | Matthew 15:8–9 |
| | Mark 7:6–7 |
| 29:14 | 1 Corinthians 1:19 |

| | |
|---|---|
| 40:3–5 | Luke 3:4–6 |
| 40:3 | Matthew 3:3 |
| | Mark 1:3 |
| | John 1:23 |
| 40:6–8 | 1 Peter 1:24–25 |
| 40:13 | Romans 11:34 |
| | 1 Corinthians 2:16 |
| 42:1–3 | Matthew 12:18–20 |
| 42:4 | Matthew 12:21 |
| 43:20 | 1 Peter 2:9 |
| 43:21 | 1 Peter 2:9 |
| 45:21 | Mark 12:32 |
| 45:23 | Romans 14:11 |
| 49:6 | Acts 13:47 |
| 49:8 | 2 Corinthians 6:2 |
| 49:18 | Romans 14:11 |
| 52:5 | Romans 2:24 |
| 52:7 | Romans 10:15 |
| 52:11 | 2 Corinthians 6:17 |
| 52:15 | Romans 15:21 |
| 53:1 | John 12:38 |
| | Romans 10:16 |
| 53:4 | Matthew 8:17 |
| 53:7–8 | Acts 8:32–33 |
| 53:9 | 1 Peter 2:22 |
| 53:12 | Luke 22:37 |
| 54:1 | Galatians 4:27 |
| 54:13 | John 6:45 |
| 55:3 | Acts 13:34 |

| | |
|---|---|
| 56:7 | Matthew 21:13 |
| | Mark 11:17 |
| | Luke 19:46 |
| | |
| 59:7–8 | Romans 3:15–17 |
| 59:20–21 | Romans 11:26–27 |
| | |
| 61:1–2 | Luke 4:18–19 |
| | |
| 62:11 | Matthew 21:5 |
| | |
| 64:4 | 1 Corinthians 2:9 |
| | |
| 65:1 | Romans 10:20 |
| 65:2 | Romans 10:21 |
| | |
| 66:1–2 | Acts 7:49–50 |

# ENDNOTES

1. I am assuming, in concert with the consensus of scholarship, that Mark's Gospel is the earliest written. I recognize that there are some difficulties with the quotation of Isaiah in Mark 1:1–2, not least that it is not Isaiah that Mark immediately quotes, but rather Malachi. On these issues, see Rikk E. Watts, "Mark," in *Commentary on the New Testament Use of the Old Testament*, ed. G. K. Beale and D. A. Carson (Grand Rapids: Baker, 2007), 111–249, esp. 113–20.

2. John F. A. Sawyer, *The Fifth Gospel: Isaiah in the History of Christianity* (Cambridge: Cambridge University Press, 1996).

3. *Biblia Sacra iuxta vulgatam versionem*, ed. R. Weber and R. Gryson, 5th ed. (Stuttgart: Deutsche Bibelgesellschaft, 2007), 1096 lines 9–11.

4. Augustine, *Confessions* 9.5.13, trans. Thomas Williams (Indianapolis: Hackett, 2019), 147. For comment on this episode, see Peter Brown, *Augustine of Hippo: A Biography* (London: Faber & Faber, 1967), 112.

5. On the history here, see James L. Kugel, *The Idea of Biblical Poetry: Parallelism and Its History* (Baltimore: Johns Hopkins, 1981).

6. Robert Lowth, *De sacra poesi Hebraeorum* (Oxford: Clarendon, 1753).

7. For a much more detailed analysis of Hebrew poetry, see F. W. Dobbs-Allsopp, *On Biblical Poetry* (Oxford: Oxford University Press, 2015).

## BIBLIOGRAPHY

Augustine. *Confessions* 9.5.13. Translated by Thomas Williams. Indianapolis: Hackett, 2019.

*Biblia Sacra iuxta vulgatam versionem*. Edited by R. Weber and R. Gryson. 5th ed. Stuttgart: Deutsche Bibelgesellschaft, 2007.

Brown, Peter. *Augustine of Hippo: A Biography*. London: Faber & Faber, 1967.

Dobbs-Allsopp, F. W. *On Biblical Poetry.* Oxford: Oxford University Press, 2015.

Kugel, James L. *The Idea of Biblical Poetry: Parallelism and Its History.* Baltimore: Johns Hopkins, 1981.

Lowth, Robert. *De sacra poesi Hebraeorum.* Oxford: Clarendon, 1753.

Sawyer, John F. A. *The Fifth Gospel: Isaiah in the History of Christianity*. Cambridge: Cambridge University Press, 1996.

Watts, Rikk E. "Mark." Pages 111–249 in *Commentary on the New Testament Use of the Old Testament*. Edited by G. K. Beale and D. A. Carson. Grand Rapids: Baker, 2007.

# MAJESTY AND MERCY

# THE MOUNTAIN OF THE LORD'S HOUSE

Isaiah 2

C. Wayne Kilpatrick

## FOCUS PASSAGE

Isaiah 2:2–4.

## ONE MAIN THING

From the time of the Babylonian Captivity God's people began to hope for a restoration of the kingdom; but their idea was that of an earthly kingdom. Before this time Isaiah 2:2–4 had foretold the establishment of a new kingdom; but this kingdom would be a spiritual one.

## INTRODUCTION

Isaiah 2:2–5 is Isaiah's first of several Messianic passages. This sets the stage for the coming of the new kingdom.

Three passages from three books of the Old Testament bear testimony to the fact that God is going to establish a spiritual kingdom in the latter age—the Christian Age. These passages are found in the second chapter of each of these three books—Isaiah 2; Daniel 2; and Joel 2: It is interesting that they are all in a chapter two. Daniel 2:44 foretells the establishment of the new kingdom. It would be in the days of the fourth kingdom in Nebuchadnezzar's dream—the Roman Empire. Joel also says that it will be established in latter times, as the Apostle Peter confirms in Acts 2: 14–21; and tells us how the Kingdom comes into existence—Joel 2:28–32. Isaiah tells us that the new kingdom—the Lord's house, will have new laws which will go forth from Jerusalem.[1]

The remainder of Isaiah's discussion concerning Isaiah is a discussion about how Judah has turned away from God unto false gods.[2] He gives a discourse in which he cries out against the prevalent vices and evils of his own day and announces the coming judgment which is going to fall on the nation.[3] So, chapters 2–4 in Isaiah detail judgments against the people who have turned their backs on the Lord, showing us that those who persist in their rebellion will receive judgment. On the other hand, we also see God's faithfulness to His promise,[4] showing the blessings reserved for those who escape the judgment that falls upon the wicked. In this prophesy Isaiah explains the purpose of the events to come in the latter days (later days or the distant future), (vs. 2). That God's people will be more than just Jews; as Peter told Cornelius— "But in every nation he that feareth him, and worketh righteousness, is accepted with him."[5] Also, all should be taught of God, (vs.3) that He might gather one people into the new kingdom. These are the central themes of vs.2-5. We shall see this as we begin to look deeper into these verses.

## GOING DEEPER

We divide Isaiah 2:1-22 into two headings: "The Mountain of The House of God" 2:1-5 and "The Day of The Lord" (6-22). That is our model for this discussion.

### *THE MOUNTAIN OF THE HOUSE OF GOD (2:1-5)*

Isaiah began here (vs. 2) with his first Messianic prophesy, and it relates to the central seat of government in the new kingdom. The center of government shall be in the "mountain of the Lord's house." This spiritual mountain shall stand out like Mount Everest stands in the Himalayas. It will be visible to all who seek it. It will be available to all nations of people, not to the Jews exclusively The ideal situation is expressed in the next verse:

> ... many people shall go and say, Come ye, and let us go up to the mountain of the LORD, to the house of

the God of Jacob; and he will teach us of his ways, and we will walk in his paths ... [6]

The people who are going to that holy place will be encouraging others to join them in that glorious journey. Sounds like evangelism is factored into this account. The people will be so overjoyed that they cannot keep this good news to themselves, thus the invitations to join the journey. They are they going up to the Lord's residence— the house of the God of Jacob. Jacob was the first man in the Bible to use the expression "the house of God."[7] At the house of God the people are going to be taught by the Master Teacher. He will teach them his ways in which they will walk. Looking ahead, verse 5 is connected to verse 3 by the thought of walking in God's ways. In this vein of thought the Apostle John wrote:

> But if we walk in the light, as he is in the light, we have fellowship one with another, and the blood of Jesus Christ his Son cleanseth us from all sin.[8]

So, walking in the light is walking in the Lord's way which gives the gift of being cleansed if they continue to walk therein. This privilege comes from being in the house of God and dwelling "in the house of the Lord forever."[9]

Isaiah continued (vs.3) by saying that this new law would go forth from Zion and the "word of the LORD from Jerusalem." This is reminiscent of the "Day of Pentecost" in Acts 2. "And there were dwelling at Jerusalem Jews, devout men, out of every nation under heaven."[10] This was the city where that event occurred. Also, Luke records: "And that repentance and remission of sins should be preached in his name among all nations, beginning at Jerusalem."[11] The gospel went forth from Jerusalem.

The Lord will judge righteously from his house. Isaiah explains this:

> And he shall judge among the nations and shall rebuke many people: and they shall beat their swords into plowshares, and their spears into pruning hooks: nation shall not lift up sword against nation, neither shall they learn war any more.[12]

A time of peace will come from the Lord to those who respond positively to God's judgment. The symbolism of beating implements of war into tools of peace is a sign of peace. The implements of war have become tools of agriculture.

We find the opposite situation in Joel's prophecy, where God addresses the wicked: "Beat your plowshares into swords, and your pruning hooks into spears: let the weak say, I am strong."[13] This was in preparation for God's judgment upon them.

Isaiah portrays the ideal situation—being in God's house, learning his ways, and walking in them.

Comparing Isaiah's and Joel's prophecies about the instruments of war and peace, we are is reminded of Paul's passage:

> Behold therefore the goodness and severity of God: on them which fell, severity; but toward thee, goodness, if thou continue in his goodness: otherwise, thou also shalt be cut off.[14]

Isaiah shows the good side, and Joel shows the evil side. We should all strive to be on the good side—walking in the light (2:5).

## *"THE DAY OF THE LORD" (6-22)*

The remainder of Isaiah chapter two (2:6–22) is devoted to that righteous judgment the "Day of the Lord." Verses 2:6–9 tell of many of God's people turned to material things and, in a sense, worshipped them and many even bowed down to images and false gods:

> Their land also is full of idols; they worship the work of their own hands, that which their own fingers have made: And the mean (lowly) man boweth down, and the great man humbleth himself: therefore, forgive them not.[15]

The next three verses (2:10-12) tell the wicked and high-minded to do as they would think — hide from

God in the rocks and dust—this is the thinking of wicked people—that they can hide from God's judgment. Isaiah say they cannot escape the judgment:

> For the day of the LORD of hosts shall be upon every one that is proud and lofty, and upon every one that is lifted up; and he shall be brought low.[16]

So, God's judgment cannot be avoided, as can be seen in verses (13-17) The lowly and the high-minded shall all be judged, along with the righteous. The haughty high-minded, the men of Lebanon, Bashan, Edom, Judah, Phoenicia, etc., shall all be brought low through God's righteous judgment:

> And the loftiness of man shall be bowed down, and the haughtiness of men shall be made low: and the LORD alone shall be exalted in that day.[17]

God will prove he alone is the one who is exalted. He alone is the supreme one. The remaining verses continue the thought of God's judgment upon the wicked and how they shall be brought low. To those men who think they can escape Isaiah says:

> To go into the clefts of the rocks, and into the tops of the ragged rocks, for fear of the LORD, and for the glory of his majesty, when he ariseth to shake terribly the earth. Cease ye from man, whose breath

is in his nostrils: for wherein is he to be accounted of?[18]

Thus, the New Kingdom will not be a place for those who refuse to humble themselves, refuse to be taught of God, and do not walk in his ways. They will be rejected. The New Kingdom and its citizens is the theme of Chapter two. At last, Isaiah's first great Messianic prophecy comes to its close. What Jeremiah said sums up Isaiah's first Messianic prophesy: "And they shall be my people, and I will be their God.[19]

## APPLICATION

There are two themes given in this text.

First: That God's new kingdom will be established as a spiritual kingdom, and not an earthly kingdom as Israel thought down to the death of Christ. Even the disciples still misunderstood after more than three years of being with Christ. "When they therefore were come together, they asked of him, saying, Lord, wilt thou at this time restore again the kingdom to Israel?"[20] In this kingdom the people would be taught by God concerning his ways and the people would walk in them. We are to walk in God's way which is in the light. "O house of Jacob, come ye, and let us walk in the light of the LORD."[21]

Second: The Day of the Lord will be a day of judgment and retribution on those who refuse to accept

God's way and to walk in it. The last sixteen verses discuss this judgment, which was to be in the last days. We cannot escape that judgment. Thus, we must be prepared—"... be thou faithful unto death, and I will give thee a crown of life."[22]

## CONCLUSION

Isaiah's Messianic Prophesy combined with Daniel 2:44 and Joel 2:28–32 tell us at what time the kingdom was to be established, how it was going to come into existence, and from where the Law would go forth. All people had an invitation to humble themselves and become citizens. The kingdom would be established as a spiritual kingdom. It would not be an earthly one. It would be in the time of the Romans (Nebuchadnezzar's fourth kingdom in his dream Daniel 2:44) and stand forever. It would be ushered in with the Holy Spirit, Joel 2;28–32. The new law would go forth from Jerusalem, Isaiah 2:3. All of this was fulfilled on Pentecost in another chapter 2—Acts 2:1–47. The new kingdom was established, the new law was announced from Jerusalem, and it was brought in by the Holy Spirit coming upon the Apostles. All was fulfilled on that day nearly two thousand years ago. The new kingdom was the church—I Thessalonians 2:12; Colossians 1:13; and Revelation 1:9. In all cases these passages are referring to the church. In those last days men will no longer have to pray "Thy kingdom come"—it will have already come!

## DISCUSSION QUESTIONS

1. What other prophet gave the same prophecy as Isaiah, but not verbatim?
2. Who could be a part of this new kingdom?
3. What was the Day of the Lord?
4. Can anyone escape the judgment of God?
5. What other books have a chapter 2 that relates to the establishment of the kingdom?

## ENDNOTES

1. Isaiah 2:2–5 KJV
2. Isaiah 2:6–22 KJV
3. Isaiah 2:2–5:30 KJV
4. Isaiah 4:2–6 KJV
5. Acts 10:35 KJV
6. Isaiah 2:3 KJV
7. Genesis 28:17 KJV
8. 1 John 1:7 KJV
9. Psalm 23:6 KJV
10. Acts 2:5 KJV
11. Luke 24:47 KJV
12. Isaiah 2:4 KJV
13. Joel 3:10 KJV
14. Romans 11:22 KJV
15. Isaiah 2:8–9 KJV
16. Isaiah 2:12 KJV

17. Isaiah 2:17 KJV
18. Isaiah 2:21–22
19. Jeremiah 32:38 KJV
20. Act 1:6 KJV
21. Isaiah 2:5 KJV
22. Revelation 2:10 KJV

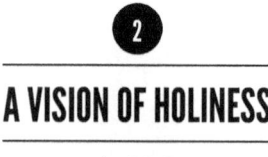

# A VISION OF HOLINESS

## Isaiah 6

### W. Kirk Brothers

## FOCUS PASSAGES

Isaiah 6:1–13

> In the year of King Uzziah's death I saw the Lord sitting on a throne, lofty and exalted, with the train of His robe filling the temple (Isa 6:1).

## ONE MAIN THING

Seeing God should lead to self-evaluation and service.

## INTRODUCTION

What we see and experience often shapes what we believe and do. One person may decide to be a physical therapist because of receiving therapy for a football injury and another may decide to be a doctor because of seeing her mother serve as a family doctor. Hebrews 11 is often called "The Faith Hall of Fame." Verses 37–38 summarize many of these heroes by stating,

> They were stoned, they were sawn in two, they were tempted, they were put to death with the sword; they went about in sheepskins, in goatskins, being destitute, afflicted, ill-treated (*men* of whom the world was not worthy), wandering in deserts and mountains and caves and holes in the ground.

Notice the phrase "they were sawn in two" in verse 37. Craig Keener notes that a popular Jewish tradition said that Isaiah hid from the wicked King Manasseh in a tree and the king cut Isaiah and the tree in half (*IVP Background Commentary*, Accordance). If this tradition is accurate, it is another example of the tremendous price that many prophets paid for proclaiming God's truth. In Isaiah 6, God declared to Isaiah that he would preach to a people who would keep listening but not perceive what they were hearing (cf. Isa 6:9). This rejection of Isaiah's message is referred to in all four gospels and in the book of Acts and applied to the rejection of Jesus and the message of salvation. What motivation would cause someone to commit to preaching a message that would be rejected? What might motivate a person to do something that would cost him (or her) his life? Isaiah would likely respond to my question by saying, "I saw the Lord!"

## GOING DEEPER

As Isaiah described the vision that propelled him to prophesy, he puts it during the death year of the Judean king, Uzziah. This 10$^{th}$ king of Judah had a very successful career and was largely faithful to the Lord. The key prophet during his reign was Zechariah (2 Chr 26:5). Late in his life, he violated God's will by offering incense on the Lord's altar and was struck with leprosy. He died around 740 BC. It was a tumultuous time. Not only was Judah losing a good king, but the Assyrian Empire was becoming a threat under the leadership of Tiglath-Pileser III (cf. *New Unger's Bible Dictionary*, *IVP Background Commentary*, Accordance).

*The Throne—I Saw the Lord*

During this time in which a good king was leaving and an evil king was coming, it is fitting that Isaiah saw the Great King of Heaven on a throne "lofty and exalted." One might wonder how Isaiah could see the Lord. God told Moses that no man could see His face and live (Exod 33:20). It seems that Isaiah was having a vision, he was not actually in God's presence. It is worth noting that the seraphim before the throne used two wings to cover their eyes. It is also interesting that according to John, Isaiah actually saw God the Son, not the Father, in his vision (cf. John 12:37–43).

Now we move to the phrase "lofty and exalted." The higher the throne, the greater the splendor. The wealthy king, Solomon, had a magnificent throne at the top of six steps:

> Moreover, the king made a great throne of ivory and overlaid it with pure gold. *There were* six steps to the throne and a footstool in gold attached to the throne, and arms on each side of the seat, and two lions standing beside the arms. Twelve lions were standing there on the six steps on the one side and on the other; nothing like *it* was made for any *other* kingdom (2 Chr 9:17).

Yet, his throne paled in comparison to the Lord's throne.

The imagery found here is both of a throne-room and a temple. This is appropriate, since God is a king (cf. Isa 24:23, 32:1) and the tabernacle and temple were described as His throne room (Exod 25:10–22, 2 Chr 28:2, Ps 132). You see a theme of fullness running through the section (cf. 6:1, 3, 4). There are also emphases on greatness, splendor, and holiness. Imagery of smoke and rumbling is reminiscent of God's coming down on Mount Sinai (cf. Exod 19:16–20). This is the only place in Scripture in which heavenly beings are described as "Seraphs." The name means "burning ones/serpent" and may allude to a brightness that was associated with them (cf. Kohlenberger & Mounce

*Hebrew-Aramaic Dictionary*, Accordance). These magnificent creatures covered their feet in homage and humility, covered their eyes because of the brightness of His glory, and hovered with two-wings in readiness to serve. Their threefold repetition of "holy, holy, holy" is likely to emphasize the fullness of the Lord's holiness. We find a similar repetition coming from the six-wing creatures around the throne in Revelation 4:8. It can give one chills to think of their powerful voices echoing back and forth to one another in the great throne chamber of the King.

*The Altar—A Man of Unclean Lips*

His vision of the magnificent Lord on the throne, compelled Isaiah to look at himself and the nation more closely. He was overwhelmed with a sense of unworthiness. Isaiah 1–5 described God's coming judgment upon Israel. Their sins stood in stark contrast to God's holiness. Isaiah may have referred to unclean lips because the vision was of the temple, the place where God's people should worship. It could also be an allusion to his role as prophet or spokesperson for God. In either case, he realized that he and the nation were unworthy. I am reminded of the reaction of Peter in Luke 5:8 when Jesus miraculously multiplied the catch of fish, "Go away from me Lord, I am a sinful man!"

God's forgiveness is symbolized by one of the Seraphim taking a coal from the altar to purify Isaiah's lips (ironic when one considers that King Uzziah was made a leper for unauthorized access to the altar of incense). Because of this cleansing, Isaiah was then ready both to worship and to proclaim the Lord's will. I am reminded of the Day of Atonement which is described in Leviticus 16. Before the high priest could offer sacrifice for the children of Israel, he must first offer sacrifice for his own sins and the sins of his family (cf. Lev. 16:6).

*The World—Who Will Go for Us?*

There are times in Scripture when we are able to listen in on heavenly conversations (cf. Gen 1, Job 1–2). One of those times is here in Isaiah 6:8, "Whom shall I send, and who will go for Us?" The word "us" in this verse could refer to the heavenly host surrounding the throne, the Divine Trinity, or it could be a rhetorical device ("thinking out loud" to compel Isaiah to take action). The New American Standard Version and the New King James Version, for example, capitalizes "Us" to show that the translators believe the Lord is talking to divine beings. The ESV, on the other hand, does not capitalize the word "us."

Isaiah's appropriate response is, "Here am I. Send me!" (6:8). This vision helps both the ancient and modern reader to understand the motivation behind Isaiah's prophetic ministry. We see a similar vision for Ezekiel in chapter one of his book. These men did not arbitrarily decide to preach and prophesy. They were responding to a divine call. They saw the Lord!

## APPLICATION

There are many applications that might be made from this chapter, but here are a few that stand out to me. The first relates to worship and Bible study. When we worship God and study His word, we have an opportunity to see the greatness and grandeur of God. We frequently miss opportunities to see His glory. Once we grasp his greatness, it will change us forever. The second take away is that seeing the glory of God should cause us to see our own fallenness more clearly. We are unworthy to be in a relationship with the Savior on the throne. We are all unclean. Yet, we have been cleansed by the blood of the Son. A third application might be that seeing our unworthiness can help us to understand God's grace more clearly and can fill us with an overwhelming sense of gratitude. Finally, seeing God should inspire us to follow Isaiah's example and answer God's call to go into the world and serve in His name.

## CONCLUSION

There are certain things, once you have seen them, you can never be the same again. For Isaiah, it was seeing the Lord on His throne. Throughout the rest of his prophetic book, he repeatedly referred to the majesty of his God (cf. Isa 37:16, 40:12–26, and 57:15). He never forgot! If he did die by being sawn asunder inside a tree, maybe his last thoughts were not of death and despair but of the Lord's glory and greatness. Maybe his soul was buoyed by a desire to return to the heavenly throne room. Maybe the sound of the saw on wood was drowned out in his mind by the echoing call of the seraphim, "Holy, Holy, Holy is the Lord of hosts, The whole earth is full of His glory" (Isa 6:3). I pray that through the eyes and words of Isaiah we can catch a glimpse of the greatness and grace of our Lord and that we never forget what we saw.

## DISCUSSION

1. What would it take for you to be willing to die for Jesus?
2. How does John's reference to Jesus being the one Isaiah saw, impact how you view this passage?
3. Discuss the fact that God called Isaiah to preach to a people that would not listen and the implications for our answering God's call to service today?
4. What are some things that keep us from grasping God's greatness?
5. What is one thing you learned in this lesson that you had never considered before?

## 3

# THE COMING KING

Isaiah 7:14, 9:6–7, 11:1–10

**Ed Gallagher**

### FOCUS PASSAGE

Isaiah 11:1–10

### ONE MAIN THING

The recognition of Jesus as the long-expected king is essential to the good news that he proclaimed.

### INTRODUCTION

The world is always full of terrible political leaders. I have no fear that such a comment will become outdated, that someone reading this lesson in a few years will find that the world at that time is actually full of wonderful leaders of nations. There might be a different cast of characters, and the nations ruled by the worst offenders might change—so I won't list here the nations that I think have the most terrible leaders—but the world will never have a moment in which awful political leaders are not prominent. Even the countries that we consider the best countries in the world (no list of those either!), the most responsible nations, are filled with idiotic and morally depraved leaders. Is that too harsh? I don't think so.

What kind of leaders do we want? Are there examples of good leaders in the history of—let's say—America? I am not a historian of the United States, so my opinion doesn't count for much, but I agree with the consensus that George Washington is one of the greatest presidents. Recently some Americans have threatened to tear down the monuments dedicated to Washington. I don't know how you feel about such attacks on the memory of America's first president, but let me go on record as saying that the reasons people don't like Washington are good reasons! He did some really wonderful things, and some that were not. (He owned slaves, many of them.) The point I'm trying to make is not that Washington deserves no statues, but rather that he was perhaps the greatest president America has ever seen, and he was nowhere close to the ideal political leader. Thomas Jefferson wrote in the Declaration of Independence words that are wonderful and inspiring and have put pressure on Americans for hundreds of years to live up to those lofty sentiments, and Jefferson himself was a hopeless sinner. I don't mean that Washington and Jefferson were our worst presidents, but our best leaders, maybe the best we will ever experience, and they were in many ways terrible. The best that we can put forward is deeply flawed.

We want leaders to bring justice and righteousness, to help those who are oppressed, to rid our society of wickedness, to offer us protection, to ensure peace. Our best leaders succeed very imperfectly in only some of these ideals, and make no progress or even attempt in other aspects. Ancient Israel experienced its share of terrible kings who cared little for peace and justice, but Isaiah promised that a king was on his way who would represent all that Israel (and we) ever hoped for in a leader.

## GOING DEEPER

Isaiah 11 is a messianic passage, meaning that it describes the appearance of an ideal king in the future. The passage does not use the Hebrew term "messiah" (*mashiaḥ*). In fact, though the term "messiah" appears thirty-eight times in the Hebrew Bible,[1] it hardly ever refers to what we think of as the Messiah. The Hebrew term itself means "anointed," and it sometimes refers to the priest,[2] usually to the king currently on the throne of Israel.[3] Daniel's prophecy of the Seventy Weeks (Dan 9:24–27) contains the term twice, but the passage is obscure and its meaning has always been debated. The bottom line is that the passages in the Hebrew Bible that use the term "messiah" are not the passages that actually talk about "the Messiah." So why do we use the term "messiah" to talk about a coming king when the Old Testament does not?

The answer is because of the New Testament. The term *christos* (χριστός) appears in the New Testament 529 times.[4] This word (related to *chrio*, χρίω, "to anoint") also means "anointed," so it is the Greek equivalent of the Hebrew term "messiah."[5] It's because the New Testament constantly refers to Jesus as the Christ, "the anointed one," that we refer to him as the Messiah, "the anointed one." Since the Hebrew Bible uses the term "messiah" ("anointed") most often to refer to a king, that is also what ancient Jews and Christians usually meant with the terms "messiah" and "christ." If we are to understand the expectation for a messiah in the ancient world, we need to look at the passages in the Old Testament that promise the coming of an ideal king (even though these passages do not use the term messiah). There are several such passages, and perhaps chief among them is Isaiah 11.[6]

How do we know that Isaiah 11 is talking about an ideal future king, a messiah? It doesn't use the word "messiah," and it doesn't even use the word "king" or "kingdom." Neither does it talk about David, as some other messianic texts do (e.g., Ezek 34:23–24; 37:24–25). But Isaiah 11 does mention the name Jesse, and the only Jesse in the entire Bible is the father of David (see especially 1 Sam 16). In fact, David was sometimes just called "the son of Jesse" (1 Sam 20:27, 30–31; 22:7–13). So when Isaiah predicts a "shoot" from the "stump of Jesse," he must be thinking about David's father, and the subject of our chapter must be kingship.

Notice that this king will be a shoot from the "stump" of Jesse. Isaiah is talking about David's family as if it is a tree, and we are looking forward to a new shoot from that tree, but the shoot is going to need to grow up from the stump of the tree. It sounds like the tree itself is going to be cut down. Isaiah seems to be predicting a time after the current dynasty descended from David will already have ended. Remember that during the days of Isaiah, the Davidic dynasty was still on the throne; King Ahaz (Isaiah 7:1–2) was a part of that dynasty. But someday, Isaiah predicts, that dynasty would be reduced to a stump, and then a new shoot would grow. In other words, the current line of kings in Isaiah's day would not fulfill Israel's hopes. Just as we have political rulers that routinely fail to bring peace and justice, so also Israel. The Davidic dynasty would need to be chopped down, and once that happens— once the promise to David for a perpetual dynasty (2 Samuel 7:12–16) seems most in jeopardy of failing— only then would the shoot appear and the promise to David would bear fruit.

What kind of king will this shoot be?

- The Spirit of the LORD (YHWH) will be on him (v. 2). This Spirit will grant wisdom to the king. Previously, Solomon had been renowned as Israel's wisest king (1 Kgs 3), but the description of the coming king suggests one greater than Solomon (cf. Matt 12:42; Luke 11:31).

• He will be just. He's not going to give preferment to his friends, or ignore the cause of the oppressed, as political leaders do routinely. This king will "not judge by what his eyes see or decide by what his ears hear" (v. 3), which sounds odd, but it may be reminiscent of the Lord's instruction to Samuel: "for the LORD does not see as mortals see; they look on the outward appearance, but the LORD looks on the heart" (1 Sam 16:7). Presumably, the fact that this king will not judge by what he sees means that he will judge according to facts and not his own desires. The shoot from Jesse's trunk will "judge the poor" (v. 4), that is, grant justice to the poor. On the other hand, he will "kill the wicked."

• He will bring peace (vv. 6–9). Animals who are natural enemies will end up not fighting but enjoying meals together. Snakes will be so tame that a nursing child will play with them. The description here sounds somewhat like the Garden of Eden, where the animals offer no threat to Adam and Eve. This description of peace is repeated later in Isaiah (65:25), where it is a part of the New Heavens and New Earth (65:17). It is not clear to me what precisely we're supposed to understand by Isaiah's description of peace among animals and people. I have heard the interpretation that the animals represent different types of people, and so this vision is fulfilled in the church, but that doesn't sound right to me. I think we're still looking forward to the complete fulfillment of this vision. But however we're supposed to understand the details of verses 6–9, what is clear is that the coming king will bring peace on earth (cf. Luke 2:14).

Wisdom, justice, and peace—sounds not only wonderful but different from any ruler we've ever seen. In fact, it does not sound like any human ruler at all, but a perfect king. It sounds like Jesus. Not only does the New Testament constantly speak of Jesus as the Christ (= Messiah), as we've already seen, but it also quotes this specific passage as having found fulfillment through Jesus. In a string of quotations from the Old Testament (including Ps 18:49; Deut 32:43; Ps 117:1), Paul concludes with Isaiah 11:10 (Rom 15:7–13), interpreting all of these passages as reflecting the promises God has made to the nations (the Gentiles) and which have now been realized through the Messiah. "For I tell you that Christ has become a servant of the circumcised on behalf of the truth of God in order that he might confirm the promises given to the patriarchs, and in order that the Gentiles might glorify God for his mercy" (Rom 15:8–9). Of course, those "promises given to the patriarchs" include preeminently that the patriarchs and their seed would be bring blessing to all nations (cf. Gen 12:3; Gal 3:8, 15–16), and Paul says that Isaiah 11 speaks precisely to this theme.

## APPLICATION

One day Jesus took his disciples to Caesarea Philippi,[7] about 35 miles north of their usual stomping grounds around Capernaum. He asked them a question: "Who do people say I am?" After hearing their report of the popular opinion about him, Jesus asked about their own view: "Who do you say that I am?" Peter famously responded, "You are the Christ" (Mark 8:29).[8] It is a turning point in the Gospel, and Jesus immediately began teaching his disciples about his upcoming suffering, death, and resurrection (Matt 16:21; Mark 8:31; Luke 9:22). Now that his disciples had confessed him as Christ, Jesus began to reveal to them the type of Christ he was (a suffering one, against expectations).

What did Peter mean by calling Jesus "the Christ"? What is a Christ? As we have seen, the title (or honorific)[9] "Christ" was often imagined by ancient Jews to be related to the concept of "king"; the Christ was supposed to be a king.[10] We can easily relate this idea to other elements of the New Testament's portrait of Jesus. The very first verse of the New Testament (in the traditional arrangement) labels Jesus as the Christ, the son of David, the son of Abraham (Matt 1:1). While Abraham was the father of the entire nation of Israel, David was the preeminent king, the head of the dynasty of kings. By calling Jesus "son of David," he means that he is in that same dynasty, he is a king like David. The Gospels show that Jesus announced the coming of a kingdom: "The time is fulfilled, and the kingdom of God has come near" (Mark 1:15). Matthew's Gospel shows Jesus, after the resurrection, beginning his final instructions to his apostles with the declaration: "All authority in heaven and on earth has been given to me" (Matt 28:18). Jesus is king.

The emphasis on Jesus as Messiah, as king, as Lord, continues past the Gospels. Peter's first sermon in Acts builds up to the pronouncement that Jesus is both Lord and Christ (Acts 2:36). While declaring Jesus "Lord" has other implications that we cannot explore here,[11] it is related to the idea of Jesus as the anointed king: both declarations mean that Jesus is in charge. While Paul in Acts tried to convince Jews that Jesus was the Christ (Acts 17:3; 18:5; cf. 18:8), in his letters Paul acknowledges that the confession of Jesus as Lord is basic to the Christian faith (Rom 10:9) and will be voiced by every tongue (Phil 2:11).

Do you want a king? Americans would usually answer this question in the negative. (Pardon me, please, non-American readers, for focusing on the situation in America for just a moment.) Indeed, the framers of the American Constitution designed it to limit the power of any particular branch of government, with the idea that a bad man elected to the office of the president would thus be checked in his evil plans. I think most people would say that the Constitution has done an amazingly good job at accomplishing this design. To say it again, the Constitution assumes that people are greedy and selfish, and so it aims to prevent elected officials from ruining everything, by limiting their power. But what if the person in charge is not greedy and selfish, but actually righteous and peace-loving and, well, perfect? Then maybe we wouldn't want a system in place to limit his power. Then maybe we would want him to be king.

Jesus the Christ is the king, the shoot from Jesse's stump, the one with authority in heaven and on earth. Isaiah 11 provides a description of the type of king the Messiah would be: peaceful, righteous, wise. While we await the complete fulfillment of Isaiah's ancient vision, when we will fully enjoy the peace and security of the Messiah, we who are a part of his kingdom already rejoice at his coming.

## CONCLUSION

Every human ruler is necessarily flawed, some worse than others. We experience the problems with such political leaders in our day, just as Israel did. I should say, every human ruler is flawed ... except one. The human named Jesus of Nazareth, the Word-become-flesh (John 1:12), is the shoot from Jesse anticipated by Isaiah so long beforehand. Isaiah 11 helps us to understand the identity of our Lord, who he is, and the nature of the kingdom of which we are a part. Isaiah 11 fills our minds with the hoped-for images of the Messiah's full reign, and we sing with the psalmist, "The LORD is king! Let the earth rejoice" (Ps 97:1).

## DISCUSSION QUESTIONS

1. How do you think Isaiah 11:1–10 helps us understand the identity of Jesus?
2. What parts of this vision in Isaiah are difficult for you to understand in light of Jesus?
3. Are there parts of Isaiah 11:1–10 that you think may have contributed to the expectations of the messiah in first-century Judaism that made it hard for some Jews to accept Jesus in that role?
4. What do you make of the vision of peace in Isaiah 11:6–9? Is that a literal description of a world that people will experience sometime? Is it a symbolic description of something? Of what?
5. Do Christians talk enough, or too much, about Jesus as Christ (messiah), or king? Should this image of Jesus influence our perceptions of him more, or less? What other images of Jesus are as important?

## ENDNOTES

1. Not counting 2 Samuel 1:21, where the term does appear in the standard edition of the Hebrew Bible (BHS) but should be corrected to *mashuaḥ* in agreement with other medieval Hebrew manuscripts; see J. J. M. Roberts, "The Old Testament's Contribution to Messianic Expectations," in *The Bible and the Ancient Near East: Collected Essays* (Winona Lake, IN: Eisenbrauns, 2002), 376–89, at 377.

2. Leviticus 4:3, 5, 16; 6:15. For the anointing of priests, see Exod 28:41; 30:30; 40:15; Num 3:3; 35:25.

3. 1 Samuel 2:10; 35; 12:3, 5; 16:6; 24:7; 11; 26:9, 11, 16, 23; 2 Samuel 1:14, 16; 19:22; 22:51; 23:1. There are further instances in Psalms and elsewhere.

4. It is also true that some ancient Jewish literature outside the Bible used the term "messiah" in talking about a coming king; for a list of such passages, see Matthew V. Novenson, *Christ among the Messiahs: Christ Language in Paul and Messiah Language in Ancient Judaism* (Oxford: Oxford University Press, 2012), 34 n. 1. My assumption is that the New Testament has influenced our language more than these other ancient Jewish texts.

5. The Septuagint usually uses *christos* as the translation for *mashiaḥ*; for discussion of exceptions, see Novenson, *Christ among the Messiahs*, 49 n. 68.

6. For brief discussion from a modern, critical perspective, see Roberts, "Old Testament's Contribu-

tion to Messianic Expectations," who accepts as "messianic" the following passages: Isaiah 11; 32:1–8; Jeremiah 23:5–8; 30:9; 33:14–26; Ezekiel 17:22–24; 34:23–24; 37:15–28; Hosea 3:5; Amos 9:11–12; Micah 5:1–5; Zechariah 9:1–10. According to Novenson, *Christ among the Messiahs*, 57–58, Isaiah 11 is one of the passages that shaped the concept of the messiah in Second Temple Judaism, along with Genesis 49:10; Numbers 24:17; 2 Samuel 7:12–13; Amos 9:11; Daniel 7:13–14. Passages that clearly rely on Isaiah 11 as a messianic text include *Psalms of Solomon* 17:21–32; *1 Enoch* 48:10–49:4; Babylonian Talmud, tractate *Sanhedrin* 93b (Novenson, 59–60).

7. Matthew 16:13–20; Mark 8:27–30; Luke 9:18–20. Luke does not specify the location of the conversation.

8. Matthew's version of this incident has Peter say, "You are the Christ, the son of the living God." Luke 9:20 reports Peter's confession as "The Christ of God."

9. Novenson, *Christ among the Messiahs*, 87–97.

10. As in many areas, so also in messianic expectations, the ancient Jewish sources present a variety of views; see John J. Collins, *The Scepter and the Star: Messianism in Light of the Dead Sea Scrolls*, 2nd ed. (Grand Rapids: Eerdmans, 2010).

11. See Ed Gallagher, *The Book of Exodus: Explorations in Christian Theology*, Cyprus Bible Study Series (Florence, AL: Heritage Christian University Press, 2020), ch. 2.

## BIBLIOGRAPHY

Collins, John J. *The Scepter and the Star: Messianism in Light of the Dead Sea Scrolls*. 2d ed. Grand Rapids: Eerdmans, 2010.

Gallagher, Ed. *The Book of Exodus: Explorations in Christian Theology*. Cyprus Bible Study Series. Florence, AL: Heritage Christian University Press, 2020.

Novenson, Matthew V. *Christ among the Messiahs: Christ Language in Paul and Messiah Language in Ancient Judaism*. Oxford: Oxford University Press, 2012.

Roberts, J. J. M. "The Old Testament's Contribution to Messianic Expectations." Pages 376–89 in *The Bible and the Ancient Near East: Collected Essays*. Winona Lake, IN: Eisenbrauns, 2002.

## 4

# YHWH IS OUR GOD

## Isaiah 25

### Tim Martin

**FOCUS PASSAGE**

Isaiah 25:6–8

**ONE MAIN THING**

YHWH[1] provides salvation, support, and deliverance for his people from all enemies, including death itself.

**INTRODUCTION**

Isaiah 25 is canonically set among several oracles of judgment and redemption. Chapters 13–25 and 28–30 contain prophesied woes to come upon Jerusalem as well as several foreign powers. These include Egypt, Cush, Babylon, Damascus, Moab, and the Phoenician cities of Tyre and Sidon. Nested among these woeful declarations are chapters 25–27, which contain encouraging messages about the redemption and deliverance of Israel and Judah.

In the ancient Near East (ANE), people believed in a myriad of different deities and the particular pantheon of gods varied between nations and cultures. Despite the different titles or names assigned to the various ANE gods, they all had generally the same roles. Whether people were Babylonian, Assyrian, Hittite, or Egyptian, they all looked to their gods to bless and protect them. These gods were asked to send rain and avoid drought, provide bountiful harvests to prevent famine, bless women with fertility and not barrenness, and to keep their foes at bay or else grant military victory over these enemies. Isaiah 25, in a format similar to the psalmists, portrays YHWH, the one true and living God, as fulfilling some of these expected roles.

## GOING DEEPER

Isaiah 25 can be broken down into three portions. Verses 1–5 contain a song of thanksgiving for YHWH's faithfulness. In 25:6–8, Isaiah prophesied about a future metaphorical mountaintop banquet where the enthroned YHWH will pronounce victory over the oppressors of his people and even death itself. In the closing verses, 9–12, Isiah foretold how YHWH's covenant people will express their joy by praising him for delivering them from their enemies, typified in Moab (25:10). John N. Oswalt comments "the writer believes that God's mighty acts of judgment and deliverance will result in an outpouring of praise on the part of God's people and a humble recognition of his power on the part of those who had so fiercely exulted over God's people."[2]

Focusing on 25:6–8, recall mountaintops are where the peoples of the ANE, including Israel, believed they could encounter their deities (24:23; cf. 1 Kgs 18:20–40). In addition, grand celebratory banquets were commonly associated with military victory and the inauguration of a new dynasty or enthronement of a new ruler. In his analysis of this passage, Marvin A. Sweeney concludes "such a banquet symbolizes worship at the Jerusalem Temple, particularly since offering at the Temple altar was conceived as a meal or banquet shared by the people with their God."[3] Isaiah described a magnificent feast where the finest meats and wines would be bountifully supplied by YHWH.

Curiously, however, this grand supper was to be for "all peoples" (25:6, ESV). Also, Isaiah described YHWH removing "the burial shroud, the shroud over all the peoples, the sheet covering all the nations" (25:7, CSB). In a passage which reminds the Christian reader of the voice from the throne in John's Apocalypse (Rev 21:4), Isaiah describes how "the Sovereign LORD will wipe away the tears from all faces" (Isa 25:8, NIV). Note how these actions would not be confined to ethnic Israel. In its original context, this prophetic message was surely directed towards Israel. However, as is the case with many OT passages, there may well be a *sensus plenoir* ("fuller sense") to these verses. It is understandable how a Christian reader could even see these passages as speaking of what would eventually be accomplished through the person and work of Jesus Christ. After all, Paul informed the Corinthians Jesus's final eschatological purpose, to "swallow up death" (25:8), will be accomplished at the Parousia (1 Cor 15:26).

In the concluding verses, 25:9–12, the prophet spoke of a future time when the people of YHWH will celebrate the deliverance he provided from their oppression. Their enemies will have been "trampled down like a dunghill" (25:10, ESV) and be spread out by his mighty hands. These same hands will dispel the arrogance of these enemies and humiliate them, reducing their mighty power to dust. These passages, when read through the lens of the entire redemptive history of the Bible, are typified in the defeat, judgment, and condemnation of the eschatological beasts, false prophet, and harlot in Revelation 20:7–15.

The reader of this article should not be misled by the above comparisons to John's apocalyptic visions nor the proposal there may be a "fuller sense" to Isaiah 25. This author is unable to concretely state whether God inspired Isaiah to utter this prophecy with a greater underlying purpose which would only become evident once the mystery of the New Testament was uncovered. It is equally dangerous to assume a typological use of Isaiah 25 in Revelation, even though the Apocalypse contains more allusion, symbolism, and typology from the Old Testament than any other New Testament book. These are merely observations from the Christian perspective.

## APPLICATION

Under the new covenant of Jesus Christ, YHWH remains the same "god" as he was to the people of the Siniatic covenant. Christians must look to God for deliverance, both from their worldly enemies and oppressors as well as their cosmic enemy, Satan. God continues to serve as a stronghold and shelter in times of trouble and a supplier of needs. His people must still call on him to provide sustenance and providence, even at the simplest level.

God is also a planner, not a capricious and impetuous deity like the false gods of Babylon, Canaan, Greece, or Rome. Human beings, as the pinnacle of God's majestic creation, are not playthings, but beloved children. His plan for the ultimate salvation of his NT people, the Church, was established before the earth was even formed (Eph 1:4; cf. Matt 13:35; Rom 16:25–26; 2 Tim 1:9). The sending of Jesus Christ to reconcile sinners to him was "an act of God's faithfulness to his covenants, his people, and most of all to himself and his strategy."[4] Consider the ubiquitous messianic banquet imagery utilized by Jesus in his parabolic teachings and the "marriage supper of the Lamb" in Revelation 19:9. In line with the language of Isaiah 25:6–8, under the new covenant of Christ, all the nations are now invited to become part of God's people and attend this grand eschatological feast. The hope of all Christians lies in the resurrection of Jesus and his promise to return, wiping away death and the tears of those suffering for God.

## CONCLUSIONS

The passage being examined here is a climactic song of thanksgiving to an omniscient creator, deliverer, conqueror, and provider. God reigns over and superintends all things, including both physical and spiritual death. No earthly or cosmic enemy can defeat him. None of the false gods of the ANE or Greco-Roman world could make this clam. Neither can human hubris, wealth, or political power. For Israel, YHWH was the provider of all the things the rest of the other nations fruitlessly sought after through the gods they fabricated in their minds and with their hands. Today, God can also provide for his people if they place their trust in him, obey the gospel summons, and keep his commandments. He can be the same resource for a lost world groping for peace, hope, and stability from inadequate sources such as money, pride, popularity, and human government. Because of all these things, God remains as praiseworthy today as he was for Isaiah's audience.

## DISCUSSION QUESTIONS

1. What are some other similar Old Testament passages which also could be read with a "fuller sense" which was fulfilled in Christ under the new covenant?
2. Throughout the Old Testament, YHWH often gives promises regarding the ways he wanted to bless Israel. Discuss how these blessings were similar to the ones sought by other nations from their deities.
3. The bestowing of these blessings was conditional. What was the most important condition YHWH demanded of Israel in order to receive these blessings? Are these same conditions required to receive blessings, in this life and the afterlife, under the new covenant?
4. Talk about ways modern people seek to provide, perhaps through their own volition and ingenuity, the basic needs of life, both physical and spiritual. How can Christians

encourage one another and the lost to turn to a reliance on God and not themselves?

## ENDNOTES

1. YHWH. Tetrgrammaton. This Greek term meaning "four-letter word" refers to the four-letter name of God, YHWH.

2. John N. Oswalt, *The Book of Isaiah: Chapters 1–39*, NICOT (Grand Rapids: Eerdmans, 1986), 459.

3. Marvin A. Sweeney, "Isaiah," in *The New Oxford Annotated Bible: NRSV with the Apocrypha*, 5th ed. Michael D. Coogan, ed. (New York: Oxford University Press, 2018), 1013.

4. John D. W. Watts, *Isaiah 1–33*, WBC 24 (Waco: Word Books, 1985), 330.

## BIBLIOGRAPHY

Grogan, Geoffrey W. "Isaiah." Pages 433–863 in *The Expositor's Bible Commentary: Volume 6 (Proverbs–Isaiah)*. Rev. ed. Edited by Tremper Longman III and David E. Garland. Grand Rapids: Zondervan, 2008.

Oswalt, John N. *The Book of Isaiah: Chapters 1–39*. NICOT. Grand Rapids: Eerdmans, 1986.

Sweeney, Marvin A. "Isaiah." Pages 977–1068 in *The New Oxford Annotated Bible: NRSV with the Apocrypha.* 5th ed. Edited by Michael D. Coogan. New York: Oxford University Press, 2018.


Watts, John D. W. *Isaiah 1–33.* WBC 24. Waco: Word Books, 1985.

## 5

# GOD'S PEACE

### Isaiah 26

### Thomas Tidwell

According to Will and Ariel Durant, in their *Lessons of History*, there have only been approximately 268 scattered years without war over the past 3,421 years. For most people, a year without war is not only desirable but considered highly desirable. Perhaps a better question is, is it probable or likely that there could be a year without war in today's world?[1]

Five great enemies of peace inhabit with us—avarice, ambition, envy, anger and pride; if these were to be banished, we should infallibly enjoy perpetual peace.[2]

## FOCUS PASSAGE

Isaiah 26:1–6

In that day this song will be sung in the land of Judah: "We have a strong city; God will appoint salvation for walls and bulwarks. Open the gates, That the righteous nation which keeps the truth may enter in. You will keep him in perfect peace, Whose mind is stayed on You, because he trusts in You. Trust in the LORD forever, For in YAH, the LORD, is everlasting strength. For He brings down those who dwell on high, the lofty city; He lays it low, He lays it low to the ground, He brings it down to the dust. The foot shall tread it down—The feet of the poor and the steps of the needy."[3]

This is part of a song praising God. From Isaiah 13-24 God had inspired Isaiah to write concerning the judgments on the nations surrounding Jerusalem, and in chapter 24, Isaiah discusses the judgment on the whole earth. As this judgment took place, there would be war, fighting and destruction. It seems to be clear, as we look at the world's history, that mankind has never done well at seeking or maintaining peace. All of this is due to man's sin; to the desire of doing things our way instead of God's way; to selfishness and pride.

In Isaiah 25 Isaiah praises God for the destruction of a city, at the same time praises God for giving strength to the poor and needy. (Isa 25:3-4). He discusses that God will wipe away tears from all faces, and the rebuke of his people he will take away from the earth." (Isa

25:8). Moab is receiving the judgment, as Moab shall be trampled down under him. (Isa. 25:10).

When Moab is defeated, then Israel will sing the song of salvation as recorded in Isaiah 26. This is a song praising God for his protection (the strong bulwark and walls). The gates will be opened so the RIGHTEOUS nation may THAT KEEPS TRUTH may enter. This brings about the peace that they need.

This peace is perfect because God is the one who protects and cares for his people.

Why? "The mind is stayed on you"—we keep the focus on God when the world is at war, in disagreements, in heartache and sorrow.

When our mind is stayed on God, then we trust God to be with us and give us peace in a world that does not understand nor know peace.

God is YAH—The Lord is everlasting strength (the Rock of Ages is a marginal reading).

## ONE MAIN THING

What do we need to do to attain the peace of God that passes all understanding? (Phil 4:7).

## INTRODUCTION

Since man sinned in the garden of Eden, the world has not known peace. Peace between God and man was broken. Through the Old Testament we see example after example of man killing man, of wars and "rumors of wars;" of man's inhumanity to man.

We live in a world of diversity. Racial differences the world experiences could lead to racism, ethnic differences can lead to prejudice; political differences can lead to wars, economic differences can lead to envy and covetousness. There are gender differences which lead to problems in marriages, and in culture (how we treat one another of the opposite sex). Lifestyle differences exist and Christians are asked to give up their principles and their commitment to God to accept sin. The desire to live our lives without God and his standards has been the problem since the beginning.

It starts as children. We grow angry over a toy, or not getting our way. We try to teach our children how to work through problems, but sometimes, what they may see in our families as well as via the media, the problems cannot be worked out. Pampered, undisciplined children only want what is best for them, and selfishness reigns.

There is no place on this planet wherein man will not have problems, except for cemeteries. Problems we face stress that we will not have peace unless we are right with God.

## GOING DEEPER

PEACE MUST BEGIN WITHIN OURSELVES. How can people be at peace with anyone else until we are at peace with our Maker, and Redeemer? We come to peace by responding to God's offer of mercy and accepting his grace through our obedience to the gospel (Rom 5:1). Further, we must work on this relationship daily. Daily Bible reading and time for prayer helps fortify us as we face what the sinful world will throw at us. What did Isaiah say? "You will keep him in perfect peace WHOSE MIND IS STAYED ON YOU." (Isa 26:3). We can have peace in our souls if we let the peace of Christ rule in our hearts (Col 3:15).

So, the reason why we aren't at peace with ourselves is our battles, fights and struggles, between our will and God's will—between wanting things our way and striving to follow the Lord's way. We will not accept that we are at fault! We justify it by saying, "I made a bad choice." If it is JUST a mistake, why do we feel bad about that? We use these words because if it is just a bad choice, an oversight, or a mistake, then maybe I can fix that! By ourselves, we cannot fix sin. We want to fix ourselves by ourselves, and we can't. We need God's help.

Therefore, God must be the focus of our lives daily. Multiple things will try to distract us, but we must keep focused on God. Taking breaks throughout the day to pray and reconnect with the word of God will keep our mind on him. Dealing with the sin that comes into our lives means that we will confess and repent of the sins; availing ourselves of the forgiveness that Jesus's blood will cleanse us from those sins. This should cause peace to know that we are right with God; this should also encourage more love for him and a deeper level of commitment to the one who cares so much for us. Therefore, ". . . let the peace of God rule in your hearts, to which also were called in one body, and be thankful." (Col 3:15).

When I am at peace with God and am assured that he is with me, then I will be able to work at having peace with others.

PEACE WITH OTHERS CAN COME IF WE WORK AT IT. In the world we can have peace if we sit down and talk with those who have had a different backstory in their lives than we. We don't grasp nor understand other races because we have not been there and faced their struggles. We do not understand those who have had a different set of circumstances in their lives that placed them in a different socio-economic background. We often do not take the time, nor try to understand what another person is going through.

It is often the case that even when Christians work together there will be differences of opinion. Due to our different experiences in life, we may look at things in ways others do not. When it comes to the Bible and what God really desires, Christians should be united in seeking his will first in our lives. When both parties strive for the same goals, idealistically, we can work together for the glory of God.

> I therefore, the prisoner of the Lord, beseech you to walk worthy of the calling with which you were called, with all lowliness and gentleness, with longsuffering, bearing with one another in love, endeavoring to keep the unity of the Spirit in the bond of peace. (Eph 4:1–3)

Consider for a moment a change in the way something is done in the church. We add a song to worship; we suggest a change as to when we partake of the Lord's Supper, or we lose focus on evangelism. Striving to change things to bring more glory to God will sometimes lead to feelings of angst, turmoil, and doubt. Sometimes it seems that everyone is looking out only for themselves, and not for others (Phil 2:4). When that occurs, then it becomes a competition as to who will win or who will get their way. God's church suffers.

Every church in the New Testament had its problems. The epistles mention specific names concerning some brethren (Phil 4:2—Euodia and Syntyche; 3 John and John's problem with Diotrephes). These problems come from hearts that have not grown in the grace and knowledge of Jesus Christ (2 Pet 3:18). These problems stem from selfishness and a desire to want what we want, as opposed to what God wants and desires. If all of us would work at peace we must all desire to seek God's will first in our lives.

Peace with others is hard, but not impossible. We discussed church problems, but family problems, problems in the workplace, and in our country can all be solved, (or at least brought to closer resolution) when all men seek peace with God first, within ourselves second, then with others. We must remember that God wants all men to be saved, and Jesus's blood can save all men. God has done what he can to effect the reconciliation that we all need; we must do our part in the way he commands and desires.

When we have a problem we MUST do things God's way, and work at resolving the problem(s) in the way God has commanded. Matthew 18:15–20 tells us we talk with the brother or sister with whom we have the problem alone. If that doesn't work, we take two or three more; if that doesn't work, we bring it before the church. It may not always be possible, but peace is something for which all Christians must work.

Jesus came and preached peace to those afar off and to those who were near to God (Eph 2:17). As Christians we must seek peace with God first, and within ourselves. It is a command that we work through our problems and seek to restore relationships with those who have sinned again us. Christians must set the example of peace in our world. Will we?

## DISCUSSION QUESTIONS

1. Why is peace so hard to come by in our world?

2. Why don't we have peace in our hearts?
3. Why is it so important to be forgiven to have peace?
4. Why is it important to keep our minds focused on God? How does this help when face death, illness, or pain?
5. What did Jesus tell us to do when we have problems with our brethren? Why is this so hard?

## ENDNOTES

1. http://www.ayww.org/faqs accessed 9 23 2021 17:43.

2. "Petrarch." *The Encyclopedia of Religious Quotations*, Westwood, NJ: Fleming Revel Company, 1965), 327.

3. In this chapter we will use the NKJV or ESV for all quotes from the Bible.

## 6

# CORNERSTONE AND CROWN OF GLORY

## Isaiah 28

### Will Dilbeck

## FOCUS PASSAGE

Isaiah 28

## ONE MAIN THING

The contrast between God and human beings is often much greater than we realize. Yet God is not some transcendent deity who does not or cannot attempt a relationship with humanity.

## INTRODUCTION

Many professional sports fans watch their heroes and are sometimes tempted to think, "I could do that." Hopefully, however, this thought is merely a momentary lapse of sanity. I recently had an experience that illustrated to me that difference between a professional and an amateur. This past summer, I rode my motorcycle on a race track for the first time. After watching my racing heroes for years, I decided to try it for myself. I anticipated it would be difficult, but I was not prepared for the immensely steep learning curve.

As I tried to learn the circuit consisting of left and right hand turns along with a very long and fast straight away, I actually forgot basic maneuvers like braking and down shifting. I was truly overwhelmed. Thankfully, by the end of the day I was more comfortable and I enjoyed it. Yet it made me appreciate those who race motorcycles professionally. There is an unfathomable and unbridgeable gap between an amateur like me and the professionals.

When contemplating the greatness of God with the finitude of humans, it is easy to resort to one of two extremes. Either we assume, like Job's three friends, that God is definitely greater than humans, but perhaps the gap isn't so large. In fact, we can understand his attributes and predict all of his actions. Thus, the three friends were convinced that Job had sinned and his calamities were merely the natural outcome. Yet, in his final speech from the whirlwind, God reminds Job's three friends and the titular figure of the book that the gap between God and humans is much greater than they and we can imagine.

There is an immensely important caveat however. God is not a being who is so great and mighty that he refuses to have anything to do with us mortals. The God of the Bible is not the God one finds discussed in Aristotle. For the philosopher, God as a perfect being could only contemplate that which is perfect, divinity itself.[1] If he contemplated anything less than perfect, it would diminish his own perfection. The consequence of this idea is that God could not possibly have anything to do with the world and the inhabitants of it. Thus we have Aristotle's well-known notion of the Unmoved Mover who perpetually causes the motion of the universe.

The Bible powerfully and repeatedly refutes this notion. When the author of the fourth gospel proclaims, "The Word became flesh," in John 1:14, God's nearness to humans is startlingly affirmed. So, as with many things in life and in thought, a balance is necessary. Yes, God is transcendent and thus far above human thought and action. But, the Holy One is also interested and desirous of a relationship with human beings.

## GOING DEEPER

So what does all of this have to do with the text under discussion, Isaiah 28? Upon a superficial reading, perhaps one might answer, "Not much." However, the contrast between the frailty of human leaders and the majesty of God is striking. If one reads Isaiah 28:5–6 in isolation, he or she could easily conclude that these verses are a simple affirmation of God's perfect justice and judgment. These ideas are clearly present. Yet, there is more to it. When reading the four verses prior to Isaiah 28:5–6 and the two after it, an ugly picture is painted. Ephraim's drunkards are presented in ugly, disgusting detail.[2] The prophet describes the priests, prophets, and other leaders as making important decisions for the people under their charge while participating in alcoholic, vomit induced parties. In Isaiah 28:5, however, the prophet boldly affirms, "In that day, YHWH of hosts will be a garland of glory, and a diadem of beauty to the remnant of his people."[3] How could such a momentous change take place? The Aramaic Targum on this passage has "The Messiah of YHWH of Hosts" for the phrase "YHWH of hosts," which is in the Masoretic text.[4] It is easy to agree with the assessment of the Targum on this point.[5] Thus, God will bring about such a dramatic change through his Messiah. Yet when we look at the gospels, Jesus doesn't rule over Israel or anyone else for that matter in a way befitting Isaiah 28:5–6. Therefore, there must be an eschatological event that will ultimately fulfill this passage, and this idea can be found in passages like Matthew 25:31–46.

The contrast of Isaiah 28:1–13 between the inebriated sots who were supposed to lead Ephraim and the perfect and just leadership of God could hardly be stronger. Yet an analogous incongruity can be found in the next section of this same chapter, Isaiah 28:14–19. In this section, the disparity is between the lies and falsehood of the Jerusalem leadership and the sure foundation of God. The leaders in the capital of the Southern Kingdom were convinced that nothing bad could happen to them. Such an attitude could be a result from the thwarted attempt of the Assyrians to destroy Jerusalem in the late 8th century. The city would stand for over a century more. Perhaps this same sentiment of trusting in the temple is echoed in Jeremiah's temple sermon in Jeremiah 7. In spite of this false hope, God reminds the people that there is a sure hope, a cornerstone or foundation stone.[6] This chief cornerstone is explicitly identified with the person of Jesus in several passages in the New Testament.[7] Moreover, Jesus is referred to as the true foundation in 1 Corinthians 3:11. Yet again, the problem of how such a drastic change can occur is answered in the form of the Messiah.

## APPLICATION

It is easy to read passages like Isaiah 28 and get bogged down in the minutiae of the imagery and historical context of the prophet. Yet the application to Isaiah 28 is profound and worthy of consideration. Every four years, the citizens of our country participate in one form or another in the presidential election. In recent years, media outlets strive to convince us that every election that occurs is the most important one. Thus, supporters of both political parties vote in earnest that their candidate will be the one who brings forth the substantive changes necessary for our country's survival. Yet every election, it seems to me that there is disappointment on both sides no matter who wins. Why is this the case? At least in part, I think it is because we realize very quickly just how human these candidates prove to be. They often make decisions which will strengthen their own political foothold on various issues rather than those which benefit a large number of the people. They often mislead or flat out lie to get elected or win political points once elected. We can easily be critical of such decisions, but let us be reminded that what they are above all is human. Maybe our leaders aren't attempting to lead in drunken stupors like those of Ephraim mentioned in Isaiah 28. Perhaps their judgment is clouded from other sources such as arrogance, power, greed, and ignorance. The problem with earthly leaders is that perfect justice remains merely in the realm of the Platonic forms; it can not be accomplished in this world.

But with God, it can, and it will. The injustices in this world are many, but through Jesus, God will rectify them in the world to come. Because of the significant differences between the imperfect justice that rulers of this age mete out, and the perfect justice which Jesus will wonderfully bring to fruition, it is worth considering just how different this will be. This future justice is beautifully stated in one of the final chapters of Isaiah, 65:17–20: "See, I will create a new heavens and new earth; the former things will not be remembered ... Never again will there be in it an infant who lives but a few days or an old man who does not live out his years."

## CONCLUSION

Isaiah 28 contains two significant contrasts. The first section of the chapter contrasts the serious shortcomings of Ephraim's leaders with God's ability to execute justice and righteousness. The second portion of Isaiah 28 shows the difference between the leaders of Jerusalem who trusted in lies with the foundation and cornerstone which God will provide. God will accomplish all of these things through the Messiah. God's justice and righteousness also contradicts what we witness with leaders of our time.

## DISCUSSION QUESTIONS

1. Read Isaiah 28 again and then read Isaiah 11. How do these passages taken together help define the concept of justice?
2. Why do human leaders fail so often? How do their failures help glorify God more?
3. It is easy to place our trust in the wrong things. Can we do this spiritually? Think about how many people fall away because of a bad experience in a local congregation.

Could this be a result of trusting in the wrong thing, i.e. trusting in imperfect humans who make up the church rather than trusting in God?

## ENDNOTES

1. *Metaphysics* 12 1072b.

2. While Ephraim refers to the Northern Kingdom, Jerusalem is mentioned in verse 14. Yet some commentators think the transition could come as early verse 7. For the purposes of this essay, it matters little. For discussion, see J. Oswalt, *The Book of Isaiah 1–39* (Grand Rapids: Eerdmans, 1986), 506.

3. I am using the NRSV.

4. As H. Wildberger, *Isaiah 28–39* (Minneapolis: Fortress Press, 2002), 4–5, astutely observes about the Targum to this passage, "Those responsible for that text could not comprehend how such a radical change, as described here, could take place without the appearance of the messiah."

5. Dating the targumim are notoriously difficult. The Targum to Isaiah is part of a larger collection of Targumim referred to as Targum Jonathan. It is called by the name because in a passage in the Babylonian Talmud, Jonathan ben Uzziel is said to have written the targumim to the prophets which of course includes Isaiah. Jonathan ben Uzziel was a student of Hillel, a famous contemporary of Jesus. Most scholars doubt the

attribution of Targum Isaiah to Jonathan ben Uzziel and the other targumim to the prophets. Therefore, the dating of the text is uncertain. However, there seems to be some traditions in the text that can be dated to just after 70AD and others to later periods. For discussion of the date and of the Isaiah Targum as a whole, see P. Flesher, and B. Chilton, *The Targums: A Critical Introduction* (Leiden: Brill, 2011), 169–198.

6. The translation of the Hebrew terms in Isaiah 28:16 is difficult. For discussion, see Wildberger, *Isaiah 28–35,* 30–32.

7. Matthew 21:42; Mark 12:10; Luke 20:17; Acts 4:11; Romans 9:33, 10:11.

## BIBLIOGRAPHY

Flesher, P. and B. Chilton, *The Targums: A Critical Introduction*. Leiden: Brill, 2011.

Oswalt, J. *The Book of Isaiah 1–39*. Grand Rapids: Eerdmans, 1986.

Wildberger, H. *Isaiah 28–39*. Minneapolis: Fortress Press, 2002.

# THE REIGN OF RIGHTEOUSNESS

## Isaiah 32

### Michael Jackson

## FOCUS PASSAGE

Isaiah 32:1–2 (New American Standard Bible, 1995)

> Behold, a king will reign righteously
> And princes will rule justly.
> Each will be like a refuge from the wind
> And a shelter from the storm,
> Like streams of water in a dry country,
> Like the shade of a huge rock in a parched land.

## ONE MAIN THING

The messianic king anticipated by Isaiah's prophecy will be a righteous and just ruler who provides protection for the people.

## INTRODUCTION

Isaiah 7:14 speaks of a child who will be called Immanuel. Isaiah 9:6–7 says that this child will be called Wonderful Counselor, Mighty God, Eternal Father, Prince of Peace. The government will rest on his shoulders. He will establish and uphold his throne (the Throne of David) with justice and righteousness. Isaiah 11:1–5 indicates that the Spirit of the LORD will rest on him, and that he will judge the poor with righteousness, so much so that "righteousness will be the belt about his loins" and "faithfulness the belt about his waist."

## GOING DEEPER

Righteousness is a primary characteristic of the Messiah, so much so that it is synonymous for the Messiah himself. This is evident in Paul's descriptions of "God's righteousness" in the book of Romans in the New Testament, where God's act of sending his son, Jesus, is both an act of righteousness and at the same time *righteousness itself* being revealed. Jesus came in righteousness while at the same time revealing what righteousness is.

Paul says in Romans 1:16–17,

> For I am not ashamed of the gospel, for it is the power of God for salvation to everyone who believes,

to the Jew first and also to the Greek. For in it the *righteousness of God is revealed* from faith to faith; as it is written, "But the righteous man shall live by faith."

There is something very vulnerable about Paul's position here. I think it bears emphasis and repeating. This isn't a very popular message today, and it wasn't a popular message in Paul's day, either. It was revolutionary. When Paul says that he "wasn't ashamed of it," he means what he says, and there's a reason he says it—it could be something to be ashamed of. It is hard for Paul to understand the gospel message from God's perspective, because it meant that he had to reenvision his entire existence, including his religious past and his understanding of God. In short, the gospel changed Paul utterly and entirely, and what he's about to share with the Romans is nothing short of the very thing that turned his world upside down. Paul's cues encourage us to sit up and pay attention; we're in for a bumpy ride.

That ride begins with the juxtaposition of the righteousness of God in verse 17 versus the unrighteousness of men in verse 18. Paul wants us to know that the gospel "reveals" God's righteousness. He also wants us to know that the unrighteousness of man "reveals" God's wrath. It is significant to see what this contrast is trying to communicate. God's righteousness and God's wrath are like two sides of a coin. Paul is saying that the character of God demands justice. We sometimes think of "wrath" as anger. That isn't what Paul is describing in Romans 1:18. The wrath referenced here is scarier. It is the absence of God's righteousness. As Francis Chan has put it, "The scariest thing about God is that given enough time, he'll give us exactly what we want."

By now you know these passages well, that the root of this unrighteousness that Paul speaks of in Romans 1 is idolatry. Idolatry in the definition of Romans 1 is much more relevant a concept than we sometimes recognize. We picture ancient peoples bowing down to cows and such. And we should, since that is what happened. However, the exaltation of anything in our lives without the proper perspective of its place in God's creation could lead to idolatry in our hearts.

What I also find interesting here in Romans 1:18 is the fact that this passage mixes the past with the present in such an interesting way, without commenting much on the future at this juncture. When it says that God's wrath "is being poured out," notice that this is in the present tense, not the future tense. Paul isn't appealing to the final judgment here. He's saying that God's wrath (again, not anger, but just recompense) is manifested in the present. We aren't talking about fire and brimstone, or final judgment. We're talking about hell on earth—unrighteous people being left to their own devices and being allowed to wallow in their own depravity.

The sin of "mankind" mentioned here is that they should have recognized God and worshipped him, but they chose not to. He even says that what may be known of God is manifest within them, because God made it so. We may be tempted at this point to have wild imaginations about what Paul is saying here, or to overextend the point. Paul's argument is simply that creation was enough to reveal God, but mankind chose not to worship him as creator.

You'll notice here that Paul is trying to establish accountability. When he says that they are "without excuse," what he means is that they are accountable to God, and therefore God's wrath (remember, not anger, but just recompense) is justified. By choosing their own gods to worship, they exchanged the truth of God for a lie. Paul is intimating that this is a punishable offense, and that punishment is God's wrath.

Idolatry is the root of the problem. Once God is not recognized as God, and anything else takes the interest and admiration of human hearts, then bad things happen. Paul wants the Romans to realize that this exchange of truth for the lies of the heart has led in the past to depravity, to doing things that are not proper. In short, not recognizing God leads to sin.

Paul poses an interesting question in Romans 3:5,

> Well, if humans act against God, and he is still faithful and righteous, doesn't that mean that human unrighteousness demonstrates God's righteousness? Why does God judge us for just showing him to be righteous by our unrighteousness?

Paul's simple answer is in the form of a question: "Absolutely not! Otherwise, how will God judge the world (this was a commonly accepted point and one that Paul has already made earlier), if evil is considered good?"

All of this leads to the ultimate conclusion in Romans 3:9 that everyone: Jew, Greek, and the kitchen sink, are all under sin. Under sin means that the power of this concept of sin is so great that it encompasses everyone to the extent that they have transgressed God's righteousness in some way or another. And this transgression deserves God's wrath.

Because of sin, Paul says, the entire world is accountable to God. The Law introduces us to the knowledge of what sin is but is powerless to stop it. The Romans were to recognize that Paul's gospel is a gospel of impartiality—meaning that the same power of sin was a complete equalizer. They, like we, were destined for God's wrath. But Paul's gospel, remember, also reveals God's righteousness. While this section of Romans demonstrates the revelation of God's wrath because of man's unrighteousness in light of who God is, the next section of Romans will reveal to us another aspect of God's righteousness. God's character demands punishment and accountability; but it also demands love and grace.

This is the story of the Messiah—the one who came and revealed God's righteousness. Romans 3:21 says that just as God's wrath was revealed by man's unrighteousness, God's righteousness is revealed in Jesus Christ. The rest from this conflict of human unrighteousness with God's wrath is called *peace* in Romans and is also a major focus of the imagery in Isaiah. This reign of righteousness and the resulting peace that comes from it is available to all who believe (Rom 3:22).

## APPLICATION

This righteous character that we expect of our Messiah, we should also try to model ourselves. Knowing that God's righteousness and wrath are flip sides of the same coin is a healthy reminder that we should not be content with injustice, with sin, and certainly not with idolatry. If we truly want the peace that comes from a right relationship with our savior, we must accept that he is the revealed righteousness of God himself.

In Isaiah 32, some of the specific remedies that are mentioned that come from a reign of righteousness are that fools are no longer called noble (verse 5), speaking against the LORD will no longer be tolerated, keeping the hungry and thirsty from their needs will cease (verse 6), and slander and wicked schemes will be stopped (verse 7). As long as these challenges remain in the world, we still have work to do.

## CONCLUSION

Our Immanuel, Wonderful Counselor, Mighty God, Eternal Father, Prince of Peace, and righteousness itself have been revealed in our Messiah Jesus. May we endeavor daily to reveal God's righteousness in our own lives and experience the peace that comes from living in the spiritual protection of our Rock and Redeemer.

# THE HIGHWAY OF HOLINESS

Isaiah 35:8–10

Keith Stanglin

## FOCUS PASSAGE

Isaiah 35:8–10

## ONE MAIN THING

Take heart! God is on our side, leading us down the right path, the highway of holiness, never to stray. He has ransomed us for a reason—to be his and to dwell in his eternal city.

## INTRODUCTION

Driving in a big city can be an adventure. One never really knows what's going to happen. That unpredictability comes not only from fellow drivers—you never know for sure what they will do, whether and how they will endanger you—but also from the newly constructed designs—you never know what the engineers will come up with next. The thoroughfare near my house is a case in point. The road has three lanes in each direction. But one day we woke up, and the lanes had been narrowed significantly to make room for a bicycle lane that literally no bicyclist has ever used and would be insane to try. You hope no one drifts in the lanes that are barely wide enough to accommodate a vehicle.

Recently, I was driving in the right lane of a familiar road. As I approached the intersection that I intended to go straight through, I saw a sign, about twenty feet before the intersection, declaring that the right lane is now a right-turn only lane. That was new, and with no warning. So I was forced either to turn right or to squeeze into the left lane at the last second. Another engineering novelty in cities is the "diverging diamond interchange." At a busy highway service road intersection, traffic flows to the opposite side of the road as it crosses the highway. Drivers should pay close attention when as they go through that one. We want to trust the civil engineers, but it is hard when the traffic appears to flow less efficiently. Driving can be an adventure, and the adventure is not always good.

Such unwelcome adventure makes me long for an open road with a smooth, unobstructed path. And it happens occasionally—usually outside of the city—wide lanes, smooth pavement, no traffic, no red lights. Have you ever been on a road like that, where the way just opens? It's almost miraculous; it's like a breath of fresh air, from out of the clear blue sky. And, we may imagine, this perfect highway has only good drivers, attentive drivers—not distracted—people who enjoy what they're doing and will not put others in danger.

## GOING DEEPER

The people of ancient Judah had gone through something much worse than traffic headaches. When the Babylonian hosts conquered Jerusalem in 586 BC, they destroyed the city, plundered and leveled the holy temple, killed an untold number of Jews, and abducted an unknown number of survivors, exiling them to Babylon and throughout Mesopotamia. Not only was this a social-political crisis, but it was first and foremost a religious crisis. The Jewish people were understandably devastated by these events, and they questioned everything, including whether there was a future for them as God's people.

The obstacles seemed insurmountable. But a generation later, another unthinkable thing happened: The way *out* appeared. As if from out of the clear blue sky, rather than being indefinitely enslaved and tormented, they were liberated and encouraged to return to their homeland. Even if Cyrus the Persian was the proximate cause of their freedom, the Jews recognized the hand of God in this miraculous turn of events.

How did this happen? What had God accomplished? Isaiah 34 and 35 portray the scene in epic, poetic terms. In Isaiah 34, the divine warrior's march of wrath spells judgment against the nations (see, for example, Isa 34:1–2). The land of Edom will be soaked in blood (Isa 34:7). Thorns infest, and dangerous animals abound (Isa 34:13–14). Creation cries out in distress. "Nature languishes,"[1] turning against the people and even against itself.

But after the divine warrior returns in victory, after the enemies have been destroyed, there is a great reversal. Isaiah 35 is a testimony to the joy of the exiles who were rescued by God, redeemed from yet another enslavement. Brevard Childs refers to Isaiah 35 as an "elaborate portrayal of the salvation of Israel."[2] "Do not fear!" (35:4), says the prophet, for there is much to celebrate. Creation celebrates. "Nature flourishes and luxuriates."[3] The desert blossoms. Rivers run through dry land. Dangerous animals are kept at bay. This new state of being is reminiscent of the original paradise, idyllic and Edenic. It is life-giving and life-sustaining, as if renewed creation.

This about-face in nature is evident also in the reversal and healing of human disease and disability. Exile has been hard on God's people. But the blind, the deaf, the lame, and the mute—they will all be made whole (35:5–6).

And then a highway will appear. A trail through the desert opens up. What is this highway? How is it described? It is the way out, the exodus, the way back home.[4]

First of all, it is called the way of holiness. It is holy because of the people who are traveling on it. It is not meant for the unclean or the foolish. It is for the redeemed, those ransomed by God, those who have obeyed his call. But it is holy primarily because of who paved the way—God. The fact that the travelers are "redeemed" implies that these people were in a situation from which they could not rescue themselves.[5]

Second, the highway is safe and secure. No lion or ravenous beast will be on this road. Travelers will not have to be on the lookout for constant threats to their well-being. There will be no more surprise attacks. Defensive driving is always good, but it may not even be necessary on this highway. It is comforting not to worry about external threats.

Third, the end or goal of the road is described. This is a road that leads to a specific destination: They are marching to Zion. This is a road of return from exile. Because of the nature of this highway and especially its destination, the journey is joyful. The pilgrims are filled with joy, overtaken not by enemies or beasts, but overcome with gladness and singing, worshiping as they approach God's holy city. Jerusalem had been laid low, but now is Zion exalted in glory.

This prophecy refers perhaps somewhat literally to the road taken through the desert back to Jerusalem, the way of salvation that was opened to the Jews to return home from exile. Perhaps this highway also refers to the whole process by which they would return to God. The way was opened to redemption and new life, a new start as God's renewed covenant people. And if Jerusalem could be repopulated by nothing but holy worshipers, then perhaps there would be no more exile, no more estrangement from God. This text overflows with hope and assurance for the new thing God is doing for his people.

Among post-exilic, second-temple Jews, however, there was a gnawing sense that there were Isaianic prophecies left unfulfilled upon their return from exile.[6] They returned, but had they really seen the glory of the Lord (35:2)? They were rescued from exile, but had they been truly saved (35:4)? The healing seemed incomplete. Indeed, death, an indication of disorder and the greatest disease of all, still reigned supreme.[7] The way was open to return home, but was a literal piece of land really the final destination? Old earthly Jerusalem was not all it was cracked up to be.

Later Jewish and God-fearing readers of Isaiah's prophecies found the fulfillment they were looking for in Jesus.[8] The Gospel accounts echo Isaiah 35 in the healings wrought by Jesus, all signs of the inbreaking of God's kingdom. In the ministry of Jesus, human diseases, including death itself, are overcome. In Jesus, we have seen the true glory of God the only begotten, full of grace and truth (John 1:14). We have seen the majesty and mercy of God. In Jesus the Messiah, we have experienced true salvation, rescued from all the enemies of God.

Even now, we live in an intermediate period between the first and second coming of Christ, when the kingdom has already come, but it has also not yet come in its fullness and eternal glory. Does it feel like we have been living in exile? To a people experiencing life in exile, *if* they have no direction, then they languish in Babylon, or they seek other paths that distract them or lead them astray to idols, false gods that have no power or authority. Such roads offer only obstacles, potholes, danger, and traffic going nowhere fast.

But through Jesus Christ, a way is opened, a highway of holiness is revealed, and he invites all people to follow him on that path. Jesus Christ himself, crucified and risen for us, is the highway, the way to life. On this road we are accompanied by the presence of God and of one another. This open road presents itself to us as smooth, safe and secure, and joyful, without sorrow and sadness, not because there are no bumps along the way, but because the destination is certain—it leads to the heavenly Jerusalem, Zion.

## CONCLUSION

Isaiah assures us that God always provides a way for his people. When the way *out* looks impossible, God always opens a path anyway. God carves a path through a raging sea, a fast-flowing river, or a dry wilderness. If our eyes are open to see it, God makes the desert around us bloom. He keeps the lions and enemies from doing any mortal harm. He provides a way of escape that leads to a more abundant life.

## DISCUSSION QUESTIONS

1. Have you ever driven on a road that didn't seem fit for safe travel? How did it make you feel? Have you experienced the relief or pleasure of driving on a surprisingly smooth and open road?
2. Which descriptions of the highway in Isaiah 35:8-10 stand out to you?
3. Have you ever felt like the Jews in exile—crushed, defeated, hopeless—and in need of rescue?
4. Where are you on that highway? Are you still languishing in exile, in sin? Are you traveling a path full of danger and deceit, spinning your wheels but going nowhere? Or are you on the way to wholeness and life, putting sin and sorrow behind you, looking ahead to a better city, the heavenly city? Would you be able to tell the difference between the two?

## ENDNOTES

1. This is the language of Jon D. Levenson, *Resurrection and the Restoration of Israel: The Ultimate Victory of the God of Life* (New Haven: Yale University Press, 2006), 211.

2. Brevard S. Childs, *Isaiah: A Commentary*, The Old Testament Library (Louisville: Westminster John Knox Press, 2001), 257.

3. Levenson, *Resurrection and the Restoration of Israel*, 211.

4. On the exodus motif in verses 8–10, see Marvin A. Sweeney, *Isaiah 1-39 with an Introduction to Prophetic Literature*, The Forms of the Old Testament Literature XVI (Grand Rapids: Eerdmans, 1996), 453.

5. For a succinct discussion of *gaal* "redeem," see John Goldingay, *The Theology of the Book of Isaiah* (Downers Grove: IVP Academic, 2014), 58.

6. As W. H. C. Frend put it, "The deliverance promised in Second Isaiah turned out to be disappointing." *The Rise of Christianity* (Philadelphia: Fortress Press, 1984), 15.

7. Levenson, *Resurrection and the Restoration of Israel*, 212, argues that the ultimate victory over death is implied in Isaiah 35.

8. Cf. the Christological interpretations in Eusebius of Caesarea, *Commentary on Isaiah*, trans. Jonathan J. Armstrong, Ancient Christian Texts (Downers Grove: IVP Academic, 2013), 175–78.

## BIBLIOGRAPHY

Childs, Brevard S. *Isaiah: A Commentary*. The Old Testament Library. Louisville: Westminster John Knox Press, 2001.

Eusebius of Caesarea. *Commentary on Isaiah*. Translated by Jonathan J. Armstrong. Ancient Christian Texts. Downers Grove: IVP Academic, 2013.

Friend, W. H. C. *The Rise of Christianity*. Philadelphia: Fortress Press, 1984.

Goldingay, John. *The Theology of the Book of Isaiah*. Downers Grove: IVP Academic, 2014.

Levenson, Jon D. *Resurrection and the Restoration of Israel: The Ultimate Victory of the God of Life*. New Haven: Yale University Press, 2006.

Sweeney, Marvin A. *Isaiah 1-39 with an Introduction to Prophetic Literature*. The Forms of the Old Testament Literature XVI. Grand Rapids: Eerdmans, 1996.

## 9

# GOD'S COMFORT

### Isaiah 40

### Bill Bagents

**FOCUS PASSAGE**

Isaiah 40:28–31

**ONE MAIN THING**

God delights in comforting and strengthening His beloved people.

**INTRODUCTION**

Isaiah 40 sings and soars as it extols the breadth and beauty of God's comfort for those who love Him. We cannot imagine a richer description of God's goodness toward His people. And we find this amazing in a book that so stoutly documents the fierce costs of sin.

The Book of Isaiah begins and ends with the reality of Israel's rebellion.

> Hear, O heavens, and give ear, earth; for the Lord has spoken: Children have I reared and brought up, but they have rebelled against me. The ox knows its owner, and the donkey its master's crib, but Israel does not know; my people do not understand (Isa 1:2–3).

> And they shall go out and look on the dead bodies of the men who have rebelled against me. For their worm shall not die, their fire shall not be quenched, and they shall be an abhorrence to all flesh (Isa 66:24).

As if these bookends were not sufficient, Isaiah 39:5–8 records God's promise of judgment to King Hezekiah. The bottom line is striking: Babylon will come and "Nothing shall be left …" Terrible days lie ahead.

Despite Israel's faithlessness, all is not lost. For all the just judgment and stout rebuke within this book, there remains a clear theme of hope, comfort, and redemption for the remnant who choose to love and trust God. Nowhere is that that theme clearer than in Isaiah 40.

## GOING DEEPER

Isaiah 40 begins with a shout of hope! God commissions His prophet to break out a message of comfort that flows from His majesty and extols His might. It tenderly expresses God's faithful love, offering amazing joy to all "who wait on the Lord" (Isa 40:31).

Isaiah clearly documents God's grace toward His people. Their comfort doesn't come because God has changed His nature or forgotten their sins. It comes on the heels of righteous judgment and offers new life.

The poetry of Isaiah 40:3–8 grasps both head and heart. A new way and a new day are coming. Paths will be made level and straight so that all can see the glory of the Lord. All must see that God has not forgotten His people.

Isaiah masterfully contrasts the greatness of God with the smallness and fragility of His people (Isa 40:6–30). The scope and clarity remind of us Job 38–41. "All flesh is grass, and all its beauty like the flower of the field" (Isa 40:6–7). It's gone in a breath. "But the word of the Lord will stand forever" (Isa 40:8). The contrast is clear, but it is in no sense negative. Rather, it sets up the momentous good news that comes next.

God is coming to claim His people. He's coming with His army "and his reward is with him" (Isa 40:10). He's coming for relief and deliverance. He's coming like a shepherd to care for His flock. His tenderness is matched by His awesome power.

Who can measure earth's waters in the hollow of His hand? Who can measure the heavens in a span? Who can weigh the mountains? Who can offer counsel to the Omniscient One? Combine the wealth, wisdom, power, and talent of all the nations, and they're "like a drop from a bucket" or "dust on the scales" compared to the Almighty (Isa 40:15).

Ever the Teacher, God has His prophet include a warning against idolatry, particularly against violating the second commandment of Exodus 20:4–6 (Isa 40:19–20). The Lord is too majestic to be represented by any creation of a human, even if that creation flows from a master craftsman using silver and gold. The inanimate cannot represent the ultimate Mover, the force that both created and sustains all life.

Compared to God, we are but insects (Isa 40:22). Even if a prince established a dynasty, his fleeting moment of power is less than a moment to God (Isa 40:24). Creature has no standing to question the Creator. Creature has no way to hide action, motive, or thought from the Creator (Isa 40:37–38). Creature certainly has no right to complain that the Creator has disregarded his rights or delayed his deliverance.

Isaiah's contrast between those who demand an answer from their Creator and those who choose to trust Him stands both subtle and strong. The magnificent Creator, the everlasting God, never grows faint or weary (Isa 40:28). And He never falls petty or small. The Almighty soars in grace and love as He gives power and strength to the weak (Isa 40:29). This power exceeds human imagination. If we think of it in terms of the fittest youth in prime of life, we have not touched the hem of the garment (Isa 40:30). It's not about physical prowess or athletic endurance. It's not about physical or mental stamina. In soaring climax, only poetic language can convey the spiritual reality of Isaiah 40.

> ... They who wait for the Lord shall renew their strength; they shall mount up with wings like eagles; they shall run and not be weary; they shall walk and not faint (Isa 40:31).

Who, but God, could make such a promise to a people who were about to be ground to dust by 70 years of oppression? Who, but God, would know the power of a promise to fill hurting hearts with soul-sustaining hope? Who, but God, would dare to love so fully?

## APPLICATION

We read Isaiah 40 through the lens of Romans 15:4 and 1 Corinthians 10:11. We believe that those ancient words remain God's word to His people in every generation. In many respects, the bridge of application between Isaiah's first hearers and us is remarkably short.

God has always been "the Father of mercies and God of all comfort" (2 Cor 1:3). The Lord has an amazing history of commissioning His servants to comfort the afflicted (John 14:1–3, 1 Thess 4:13–18, Rev 21:1–4). Two thoughts immediately come to mind. We are doing God's work God's way whenever we offer legitimate biblical comfort to others. In doing so, we stand in a long and loving tradition of faithful service. Secondly, each of us has received amazing comfort from God, through both Scripture and the kind words of those who are taught and motivated by Scripture.

Isaiah 40 also reminds us that the comfort of God comes with content. As powerful as God's word stands, God's word is never "just words." It flows from and is truth. When the voice said "Cry!" Isaiah asked the perfect question: "What shall I cry?" (Isa 40:6). Isaiah knew he needed to communicate spiritual content, God's truth, if he was to bless his people. That principle will stand as long as this earth stands.

Isaiah 40 reminds us that God does not comfort His people while they persist in rebellion. He does not comfort us in our sins. He comforts us when we renounce sin, amend our ways, and return to faithfulness (Isa 40:1–2). As much as God loves to comfort, He never deceives. Sin costs. It always costs more than advertised.

Isaiah 40 powerfully reminds us of the omniscience of God. He is always prepared to bless, save, rescue, and grow His people. Isaiah 40:3–5 reminds the people of God to prepare to see and to receive His blessings. God can create amazing new days for people who have the faith to receive them.

In many respects, Isaiah 40 is best read in concert with Isaiah 6, the prophet's vision of the throne of God. We know the ancient truism, "Get God right, and you'll get life right." Seeing God's power and purity, God's majesty and might, God's grace and God's goodness, sets the stage for faithful living. He knows all, so we need to ask Him to teach us. He has all power, so we ask Him to aid us. He is the ultimate leader, so we gladly follow. A huge message from Isaiah 40 is "let God be God." Our salvation is not in human wisdom, wealth, education, government, or technology. God alone is worthy of adoration and complete trust. No idol of any type must be allowed to distract us from the majesty of God.

## CONCLUSION

Isaiah 40 is an amazing song of spiritual success. It's a sweet and powerful declaration of God's fierce love. It's a moving reminder that God comforts and saves those who trust Him. It's a clear declaration that God's comfort is far more than the mere endurance of barely hanging on by a thread. Ultimately, God's comfort ends in soaring strength. God's comfort ends in salvation. It ends in the peace that passes understanding. It ends with us at home with Him forever.

## DISCUSSION QUESTIONS

1. In what ways has God offered comfort to you and your family? In what ways does He continue to do so?
2. In what ways has God blessed you to offer hope and comfort to others?
3. What can we do to heighten our appreciation for the majesty of God?
4. How will it bless us to better grasp the majesty of God?
5. In what ways and through what means does God renew the strength of His people today?
6. Why does God continue to renew the strength of those who serve Him?

# BEAUTIFUL FEET

Isaiah 52:7–10

Todd Johnston

## FOCUS PASSAGE

Isaiah 52:7–10

## ONE MAIN THING

Isaiah paints an image that fully demonstrates the active greatness, power, and love of God which opens doors of new life through the missional message of the gospel, and we are called to both live in and live out this message.

## INTRODUCTION

We prefer shoes be removed when entering our home, and for good reason. What the bottom of a shoe or sandal collects while traversing the world can be gross.

Yet this grossness is nothing compared to what feet encountered during a time when "cities lacked sewers, donkeys or horses rode through them, and streets ran with filth."[1] These realities make it nearly unbelievable for anyone to claim a sight of "beautiful feet." What Isaiah demonstrates is not the sight of sightly feet, but the message of hope and joy they carried. As joy fills the hearts and music fills the lungs, I imagine a chorus of watchmen singing out, for the only response is to marvel at His Majesty!

This passage presents a people of God in exile searching for God's deliverance. Dread filled the air as the people were struck with weary souls and caught in a deep sleep in the bed of hopelessness. Their sheets filled with depression and their heads lay heavy upon the thought that their God, who once heard their cries, had now turned a deaf ear towards them. It is in this moment of distress that we see God's power. Just as Paul speaks of a God whose "power is made perfect in [our] weakness" (2 Cor 12:9), the people of Israel are awakened by a God who brings a message of salvation in the time they need it most.

While there are many things we can learn from this passage, I want to focus on three main points. First, we are presented with a God who saves. God is magnificent, awesome in power, almighty, merciful, and loving. He brings hope in a time of hopelessness, peace where there is none, strength in the midst of our weaknesses, and salvation to all. In a time when all seemed lost, God brings a message that He is still in control, and He will reign victorious for all time. Second, we learn that the message that is received is a message that we must respond to with joy and thanksgiving. The only appropriate response to such good news is to sing out and marvel at what God can do. Third, God's love impacts us in such a way that we desire to go from recipients of this message to messengers in hopes that we will be seen for our beautiful feet as we bring forth the message of God's salvation to all the world.

## GOING DEEPER

Isaiah paints the image of a messenger bringing the good news of victory and salvation from God. The watchmen and the city respond with song and rejoicing because God has seen them and determines to save them. The rejoicing continues as God roles up His sleeves showing His strength and victory. He has brought salvation to all people.

Isaiah 52:7 shows watchmen standing on post upon the wall with a keen eye outward, expecting the worst while hoping for the best. They strain forward to see a lone messenger upon the mountains approaching the city of God. They know immediately that this herald is bringing good news of victory. This is a proclamation that heralds in the new era of God's victorious claim of His people.[2] This is a fourfold message of God's bringing of peace, happiness, salvation, and victory. God is demonstrating His majesty through extension of His mercy. God had never deserted His people, even when they had deserted Him.

Zion's response is as instructed in verse one, "Awake, awake" for here comes the proclamation that "Your God reigns" (Isa 52:7); a message familiar with old practices of temple worship in song (Ps 93:1; 97:1). In verse eight, the watchmen sing joyously, their faith being turned into sight as their hope is restored having seen the "return of the LORD" with their own eyes, "for eye to eye they see."[3] In verse nine, the city reacts in similar fashion as celebration breaks the bonds of depression and singing erupts among all. Celebration of song is the response in this city of waste and ruins for soon Isaiah will tell of the God who rebuilds, repairs, and restores (Isa 58:12). Although Jerusalem is found in waste and welter now, the God whose Spirit breathes masterpiece from chaos[4] has sent His beautiful message of peace, happiness, salvation, and victory.

God brings forth His fourfold message through a fourfold method. In the second half of verse nine, God brings comfort to a people who found none, and He redeemed His prized possession who found themselves previously under the bondage of Babylon. Verse ten shows how He has "bared his holy arm," an image of the LORD rolling up His sleeves demonstrating a personal showing of strength and action.[5] Finally, God extends the message of salvation to all the ends of the earth, a message carried by the herald now and fulfilled by our

Savior (Matt 28:18–20; Mark 16:15; Acts 1:8). Surely God's provision comfort, redemption, strength, and salvation will bring about the hope of peace, happiness, salvation, and victory. It is here we see how the message (v. 7) and the method (vv. 9c–10) surround the rejoiceful response of the people of God (vv. 8–9b).[6]

## APPLICATION

Isaiah 52:7–10 is a reflective passage of the whole gospel message. Like Zion, we are lost and captive to our sin, exiled from the hope that is found in Christ. The good news is that we do not have to stay in our captivity and exile. In Christ, we have a newfound hope of salvation, a comfort of redemption. We have peace, happiness, strength, and victory. The question we are forced to ask ourselves is how responsive are we to this majestic message of mercy and grace?

In Romans 10:14–15, Paul lays out the path necessary for a person to be saved. First, we will call on Jesus to save us when we believe that He can; next, this belief can only come to those who have heard; thirdly, hearing can only occur if there is someone proclaiming the message; finally, there will only be someone proclaiming Jesus's message if they are sent. This is why Paul utters the words of Isaiah in verse 15, "how beautiful are the feet of those who preach the good news!" While this is the response of the message giver, what is the response of the message receiver? Paul quotes from Isaiah a second time in Romans 10:16 that leads to the rhetoric "hearing is not enough." He quotes from Isaiah 53:1 which prophesies that not all who hear will believe, but there will be a remnant who are responsive to the power and greatness of our God.

The response of the remnant of Zion is seen throughout the first 10 verses of Isaiah 52, and they are all responses we must have today to the same God who presents us with the same message of peace, happiness, salvation, and victory. God calls His people to awake, be clothed with beautiful garments, arise, and remove the bonds that hold them captive (Isa 52:1–2). Paul tells Christians to awake and arise (Eph 5:14), be clothed in the beautiful garments of Christ through baptism (Gal 3:27) and be set free from sin (Rom 6:7). If we are to openly respond to the gospel message, we must first awake and arise, be clothed in Christ, and remove the bonds that held us captive. We can do this because we believe having heard.

The "here I am" in Isaiah 52:6 invites the people who have awoken to welcome all who bring the gospel message. This is reminiscent of the "here I am" of Isaiah (Isa 6:8) when God sought a messenger to deliver the proclamation of exile. This time, however, the messenger brings a proclamation of deliverance. Soon the recipients of the message shall become the deliverers themselves. As Christians, we pursue a life walking by the Spirit (Gal 5:16) strong in the strength of the Lord. When the people of God are told to awake, they are also told to put on their strength (Isa 52:1). This strength is the strength that comes from the Lord, as we too are to be armed with such strength, taking up the whole armor of God (Eph 6:10–11). Truth, righteousness, faith, salvation, and the sword of the Spirit are all carried upon the feet covered with the shoes prepared to take forth the message of the gospel of peace (Eph 6:13–20). God has requested His people be sent to proclaim the gospel so that all may hear and believe (Matt 28:18–20). We proclaim having been sent.

How beautiful are the feet that continue to carry this message! A message that brings about a response of joy and singing. A message that speaks of God's power and mercy. A message that tells of God looking with favor upon His people and bringing hope of light in the darkness. Because we now proclaim this message, more will hear and rejoice and sing out as the good news is delivered repeatedly. It is a message of how God loves us so much that He continues to show us favor and grace even when undeserved.

## CONCLUSION

We prefer to have shoes removed when entering our home because we understand how easily dirt is tracked in. Our home is a place where we seek to keep free from dirt, so we take provisions and do our best to keep it out. Much like our home, as Christians we desire to keep our lives free from the stains of this world.

However, unfortunately throughout life we allow the stain of sin to enter as we find ourselves much like the prodigal son.[7] We don't like how dirty it is, but we allow the proverbial dirt of sin and mistake to get tracked in. Soon this sin can entrap us and keep us weighed down in bonds of destruction and hopelessness. In this state we could never do anything to reverse our horrid condition. However, Isaiah presents us with an image of a majestic and merciful God who can reverse, redeem, and restore us. He will make pure what we could not. He will make holy what is unholy. He will make beautiful what seems unbeautiful. Just think, the prodigal himself would have no father to run towards had not the Father first ran towards us with His beautiful feet. Praise be to this God! Praise be to our God! And let us sing joyously to the God who demonstrates His majesty through mercy.

## DISCUSSION QUESTIONS

1. What are some ways you can bring the gospel message to your community?
2. How does having the opportunity to tell others about the gospel show the majesty of God?
3. In what ways is God's mercy seen through this message of peace, happiness, salvation, and victory?

4. How does God's method of providing comfort, redemption, strength, and salvation demonstrate His majesty?
5. What are biblical ways that show we are calling on the name of the Lord?

## ENDNOTES

1. John Goldingay, *Isaiah for Everyone*, Old Testament for Everyone (Louisville, KY: John Knox Press, 2015).

2. Gary Smith, *Isaiah 40–66*, The New American Commentary (Nashville, TN: Broadman & Holman, 2009).

3. Alec J. Motyer, *Isaiah: An Introduction and Commentary*, Tyndale Old Testament Commentaries (Downers Grove, IL: InterVarsity Press, 1999).

4. Genesis 1 tells of the creation through which we see God creating beauty and order through waste and chaos.

5. Motyer, *Isaiah*.

6. Motyer, *Isaiah*.

7. Luke 15:11–32 records the story of the prodigal son who finds himself leaving the abode of his father for the lustful lure of the world. Soon, the prodigal realizes his mistake and returns to his father who shows mercy, grace, and love by welcoming him home.

## BIBLIOGRAPHY

Goldingay, John. *Isaiah for Everyone*. Old Testament for Everyone. Louisville, KY: John Knox Press; Society for Promoting Christian Knowledge, 2015.


Motyer, J. Alec. *Isaiah: An Introduction and Commentary*. Vol. 20. Tyndale Old Testament Commentaries. Downers Grove, IL: InterVarsity Press, 1999.


Smith, Gary. *Isaiah 40–66*. Vol. 15B. The New American Commentary. Nashville, TN: Broadman & Holman, 2009.

# THE SUFFERING SERVANT

Isaiah 53

Justin Guin

## FOCUS PASSAGE

Isaiah 52:10–53:12

## ONE MAIN THING

The Suffering Servant provides salvation by enduring the consequence of our transgressions and iniquities.

## INTRODUCTION

The gospel message spread into Samaria, where Philip baptized many. Amid his success there, the angel of the Lord told him to leave and preach to a man returning home to Ethiopia after he worshiped in Jerusalem. When Philip came upon the Ethiopian eunuch, he was reading from the scroll of Isaiah, and the evangelist asked the man, "Do you understand what you are reading?" (Acts 8:31, ESV). The eunuch read from Isaiah 53:7–8. Puzzled by this selfless act, the eunuch asked, "About whom, I ask you, does the prophet say this, about himself or about someone else?" (v. 34). Luke records how Philip, beginning with this text, preached Jesus to the Ethiopian eunuch (vv. 35–38).

Acts 8:31–35 is one example that connects Jesus to Isaiah's Suffering Servant in the New Testament. Matthew, Paul, Peter, and John also quote from this passage to teach about various aspects of Jesus's work, including His healing ministry, rejection by the Jews, and atoning sacrifice at Calvary. A study of this Old Testament text reveals how these biblical writers were able to connect an ancient prophetic text to the present work of Christ.

## GOING DEEPER

Isaiah 53 is the fourth song in a series of texts known as the "Servant Songs." This passage describes the Messiah's mission. Israel failed to lead the nations to the Lord (Isa 49:4). Since they did not accomplish this task, the Lord would fulfill it through the Messiah (Isa 50:2; 51:18). Approximately seven hundred years before the events occurred, the prophet predicted the life, death, and resurrection of Jesus Christ and how He would lead people to God. The guiltless Suffering Servant would die in the place of the guilty bearing the punishment of our transgressions and iniquities. As Isaiah states clearly, "With his stripes, we are healed" (Isa 53:5).

*The Success of the Suffering Servant (Isa 52:13–53:1)*

Isaiah 53 begins with two questions, "Who has believed what he has heard from us? And to whom has the arm of the Lord been revealed?" (v. 1). In the first question, Isaiah declares the successes of the Suffering Servant. In Isaiah 52:13–15, He would "act wisely" and be "exalted." His exaltation would come at a great price. The Servant would be "marred beyond human semblance" (v. 14). Through His suffering, though, the Messiah brought hope. The phrase "he shall sprinkle many nations" echoes the purifying rites Moses performed when establishing the covenant with Israel (cf. Exod 24:6–8).[1] The verb "sprinkle" occurs twenty-two times in the Old Testament. It speaks of hallowing people and things (Exod 29:21; Lev 8:11), cleansing (Lev 14:7), and atonement (Lev 16:14–16).[2] The Servant brought sanctification, holiness, and penance to a sinful people (cf. Isa 1:18). He humbled kings and shamed His oppressors (v. 15).

The second question describes the Servant's work as revealing the "arm of the Lord." The prophet previously used this image to convey the saving power of Yahweh. In Isaiah 51:9, the arm of the Lord delivered Israel from Egyptian slavery. The longtime oppressor of God's people is viewed as an ancient mythic monster slain by the power of God. Later in Isaiah 52:10, the "arm of the Lord" would bring salvation, not only for Israel but all nations.[3] How would the Lord accomplish this mission? What would the Messiah be like? Would he be a conquering mighty king? No, just the opposite would prove to be true. He lived in humiliation and subjected himself to a shameful death. Because of the nature of the Messiah's mission, the Jews of Jesus's day rejected Him. In John 12:48, Jesus quoted this passage to prove their impenitent hearts fulfilled Isaiah's prophecies about their rejection of the Christ (cf. Rom 10:16).

*The Humility of the Suffering Servant (Isa 53:2–3)*

In Isaiah 53:2–3, the prophet depicts the Servant's life as one characterized by humility and grief. He would have an unassuming nature (Isa 53:2). Jesus's teaching astonished others, but nothing about his physical appearance made him different from any other Jewish man (cf. Matt 7:28–29; Luke 2:46–47). He would be a "man of sorrows," "despised and rejected," and "acquainted with grief" (Isa 53:3). He lived in a town of no significance. Even one of his disciples would ask, "Can anything good come from Nazareth?" (John 1:45–46) His people were ashamed of him (John 1:11) because he did not represent the things which were important to them like wealth (Luke 16:14), social prestige (Luke 15:1–2), and desiring to be served (Mark 10:35–45). And, for many today, he is despised for the same reasons.[4]

*The Sacrifice of the Suffering Servant (Isa 53:4–9)*

Isaiah 53:4–9 is the heart of the passage because it encapsulates the Servant's love for lost humanity. The innocent gave His life for the guilty even though we despised and rejected Him. Notice the plural pronouns in Isaiah 53:4-6: our griefs, our sorrows, our transgressions, and our iniquities. There was nothing we could do about these burdens. It required intervention by God in the person of Jesus of Christ. What could He do? Note the verbs portraying His work. He has borne our griefs (v. 4), was wounded for our transgressions (v. 5) and crushed for our iniquities (v. 6). We have peace with God through His chastisement because the Suffering Servant tamed sin's hostility. The word "lamb" in 53:7 is translated in the LXX by *amnos*. In the New Testament, biblical writers used *amnos* exclusively to describe the sacrificial work of Jesus Christ. He was the "Lamb of God," who took away the sins of the world (cf. John 1:29).[5] There is little doubt to whom Isaiah is referring. Thus, as noted in the introduction, Philip began with this text and "preached Jesus" to the eunuch.

All of His sufferings were according to the will of the Lord (Isa 53:10). The Father did not take pleasure in seeing Jesus suffer. Instead, he delighted, not in His humiliation and death, but its benefits to humanity.[6] Jesus understood his task ended with a cross and enduring weight of sin (John 18:11; cf. 2 Cor 5:21; Heb 12:2-3). Jesus was not a martyr, nor was his death an accident. He willingly sacrificed himself to forgive us of sin.

## APPLICATION

What are we to learn from Isaiah 53 and the Suffering Servant? The primary point of the passage is clear. The Suffering Servant provides salvation by enduring the consequence of our transgressions and iniquities. It is a message of triumph. Isaiah describes our sins as "transgressions" and "iniquities." Transgression is a rebellion in apparent defiance of authority. It is an action contrary to God's standard of holiness as outlined in His word.[7] Iniquity refers to wrongdoing with the implication of guilt. It is a judicial state of being liable for misconduct.[8] Both of these words make it clear we are guilty and deserve the punishment for our transgressions. The Messiah bore the punishment for these sins. He was "crushed," "pierced," and took our consequences. Isaiah says, "The Lord laid on him the iniquity of us all" (53:6). No doubt Israel was familiar with this image. On the Day of Atonement, the high priest laid the people's sins on a scapegoat. Leviticus 16:22 says, "The goat shall bear all their iniquities on itself to a remote area, and he shall let the goat go free in the wilderness." The Messiah became the atoning sacrifice at Calvary. Paul wrote, "For our sake, he made him be sin who knew no sin so that in him we might become the righteousness of God" (2 Cor 5:21). On this point, Isaiah concluded, "Out of the anguish of his soul he shall see and be satisfied; by his knowledge shall the righteous one my servant, make many to be accounted righteous, and he shall bear their iniquities" (Isa 53:11). We are accounted righteous not because of our goodness or ability. It is through the vicarious work of Jesus on our behalf. Jesus's humiliation and sacrifice uniquely qualify him to be our Lord, Savior, and Intercessor (1 John 2:1–2).

## CONCLUSION

"Who has believed what he has heard from us?" Jesus and Paul quote this text to describe those who reject Jesus and his gospel message (John 12:48; Rom 10:16). Belief is not just mental assent to biblical principles. It is an obedient response to Jesus's saving work. When you study Isaiah 53, you are faced with a challenge—what will you do with Jesus? The Ethiopian eunuch heard the message from Philip, and he was baptized into Christ. Obedient faith continues as you endeavor to walk as Jesus did (1 John 2:5–6). In Paul's letters, you are challenged to "walk in Christ" (Col 2:6–7) and have his mindset (Phil 2:5). Jesus, the Christ, offers you grace, expects faith and demands obedience. Such a life walks in God's light and continually cleanses you from unrighteousness (1 John 1:7). Without Isaiah's Suffering Servant, none of these blessings are possible.

## DISCUSSION QUESTIONS

1. Is Isaiah 53:1 still a challenge today? Note how Paul and Jesus use it in John 12:48 and Romans 10:16).
2. Isaiah says The Suffering Servant was "despised and rejected." What were some ways Jesus endured this during his earthly ministry?
3. Matthew 8:17 quotes Isaiah 53:4. In what ways did Jesus carry out this work? How does he do this today?
4. Read Philippians 2:6–11. How does Isaiah 53 help you understand this passage better?
5. What does atonement mean? What do you learn about Christ's work in atonement from Isaiah 53? Compare it to Leviticus 16.

## ENDNOTES

1. Gary V. Smith, *Isaiah 40–66*, NAC 15B (Nashville: Broadman & Holman, 2009), 439.

2. Alec J. Motyer, *Isaiah: An Introduction and Commentary*, TOTC 20 (Downers Grove: InterVarsity Press, 1999), 375.

3. Raymond Ortlund, Jr., "Isaiah," in *The ESV Study Bible*, ed. Wayne Grudem et al., (Wheaton: Crossway, 2008), 1335.

4. Warren Wiersbe, *Be Comforted*, (Wheaton: Victor Books, 1996), 137.

5. Don Shackleford, *Isaiah*, Truth for Today (Searcy: Resource Publications, 2005), 539–40. See also 1 Peter 1:19. Warren Wiersbe notes that twenty-eight times in Revelation Jesus is described as "the Lamb" (139).

6. Shackleford, 541.

7. James Swanson, *Dictionary of Biblical Languages with Semantic Domains: Hebrew*, (Oak Harbor: Logos Research Systems, 1997), n.p.

8. Swanson, n.p.

## BIBLIOGRAPHY

Motyer, Alec J. *Isaiah: An Introduction and Commentary*, Tyndale Old Testament Commentary 20. Downers Grove, IL: InterVarsity Press, 1999.

Ortlund, Jr., Raymond. "Isaiah." Page 1335 in *The ESV Study Bible*, Edited by Wayne Grudem, et al. Wheaton, IL: Crossway, 2008.

Shackleford, Don. *Isaiah*. Truth for Today. Searcy, AR: Resource Publications, 2005.

Smith, Gary V. *Isaiah 40–66*. New American Commentary 15B. Nashville, TN: Broadman & Holman, 2009.

Swanson, James. *Dictionary of Biblical Languages with Semantic Domains: Hebrew*. Oak Harbor: Logos Research Systems, 1997.

Wiersbe, Warren. *Be Comforted*. Wheaton, IL: Victor Books, 1996.

## 12

# GOD'S HIGHER WAY

### Isaiah 55:8–9

### Ismael Berlanga

**FOCUS PASSAGE**

Isaiah 55:8–9

**ONE MAIN THING**

God's ways and thoughts are out of this world!

**INTRODUCTION**

In this critical section of Isaiah, the Lord is calling His people to return, and He is doing so with open arms. True, there is guilt, fear, and anxiety that stand in the way of the people's return, but the Lord responds, saying,

> This is like the days of Noah, as I swore that the waters of Noah should no more go over the earth, so I have sworn that I will not be angry with you, and will not rebuke you (Isa 54:9).

Isaiah 55 invites the people to believe that better days are ahead using words like, "everlasting covenant, compassion, joy, peace, singing, and an everlasting sign." However, despair and shame cause ears to hear those generous words suspiciously, especially since the world preys on trust. To this, the Lord responds with hope.

> Seek the LORD while he may be found; call upon him while he is near; Let the wicked forsake his way, and the unrighteous man his thoughts; let him return to the LORD, that he may have compassion on him, and to our God, for he will abundantly pardon (Isa 55:6–7).

The Lord's people have a decision to make at this point. Will they wholeheartedly believe that the Lord will forgive and restore or will they view this gracious offer with suspicion and doubt? Anticipating skepticism and reluctance, the Lord gives the reason behind why His grace is so different than what they may have experienced in their dealings with the world.

> For my thoughts are not your thoughts, neither are your ways my ways, declares the LORD. For as the

heavens are higher than the earth, so are my ways higher than your ways and my thoughts than your thoughts (Isa 55:8–9).

The Lord's response here is absolutely incredible. In essence, the Lord says that with the space between our physical world and the heavens, comes a difference in thinking and behavior. Simply put, if we seek to understand the Lord's goodness through the patterns and behaviors of this world, it will lead to confusion because the Lord, His character, and righteous actions are quite literally out of this world!

## Going Deeper

When God's people were led out of Egypt and were transformed into a nation, the Lord made it clear to them that He wanted a nation of influencers guided by wisdom from above. He wanted a people who would demonstrate His heavenly attributes to a broken world. Moses told the people,

> See, I have taught you statutes and rules, as the LORD my God commanded me, that you should do them in the land that you are entering to take possession of it. Keep them and do them, for that will be your wisdom and your understanding in the sight of the peoples, who, when they hear all these statutes,

will say, "Surely this great nation is a wise and understanding people" (Deut 4:5–6).

The nation's connection to a source of wisdom and understanding from beyond this world would be clearly seen if they were to follow God's guidance faithfully. The newly declared nation of Israel could now influence nations. All this was to set the foundation for the church, which would be charged with changing the world (Matt 28:18–20).

The Lord also told the people that as they set out on this new path, His love would be with them (Deut 10:14–15). This special love, traveling through the heavens, would find a home with them and would energize the nation through the difficult days ahead. The closeness would also cause the surrounding people to take notice and marvel (Deut 4:7).

Sadly, as Israel set out into the world, the strong connection with this love diminished because of sin, prosperity, worldly influences, and suffering. By the time Isaiah began calling out to the people, the world had erased the sweet memory of God's grace and love.

Isaiah 55:3 paints a heartbreaking picture of how disconnected the people were with their God. The Lord said, "Incline your ear, and come to me; hear, that your soul may live." During this time, Isaiah's contemporary Hosea would give further insight into God's call for the people to listen and return,

> When Israel was a child, I loved him, and out of Egypt I called my son. The more they were called, the more they went away; they kept sacrificing to the Baals and burning offerings to idols. Yet it was I who taught Ephraim to walk; I took them up by their arms, but they did not know that I healed them. I led them with cords of kindness, with the bands of love, and I became to them as one who eases the yoke on their jaws, and I bent down to them and fed them (Hos 11:1–4).

Despite the dire condition that the nation was in, Isaiah reminds the people that the Lord could still usher in wonderful days of restoration if they would listen, seek, and return to Him (vv. 2,6–7). The Lord closes this thought by affirming the power and trustworthiness of His commands, saying,

> For as the rain and the snow come down from heaven and do not return there but water the earth, making it bring forth and sprout, giving seed to the sower and bread to the eater, so shall my word be that goes out from my mouth; it shall not return to me empty, but it shall accomplish that which I purpose, and shall succeed in the thing for which I sent it (Isa 55:10–11).

There was no need to doubt whether the Lord would keep His word. His word was as sure as the seasons, the life-giving rain, and the harvest. The real question was whether they would stop running from God and feel the warmth of their Father's embrace once again.

## APPLICATION

How many of us can relate to Israel's struggle? How many of us began our journey into the world, hearts full of love for God and a desire to do what is right, only to stray from the path of righteousness? How many of us have experienced valleys so deep that the warmth of God's love seemed distant? How many of us have felt too unclean to believe that God would want us back? The truth is, we all can relate on some level to this exchange between God and His people.

Although there are so many places within this text that directly speak to us today, one main thought stands out as an encouragement to us all. It is the idea that no matter what happens, with God, better days are ahead. The Scriptures are filled with examples of believers that became disenfranchised and fell away. Some turned away from God because of greed and pride. Some fell away because of unbelief. God is in control, and we know that no matter what happens in this life, standing with God is the best possible place that we can be.

Paul said it this way in the book of Romans 8:28, "And we know that for those who love God all things work together for good, for those who are called according to his purpose." Just as the nation of Israel experienced deep valleys and dry seasons, we too will go through difficulties and challenges. Some of these hardships may be situations of our own doing, and others may be entirely out of our control. This passage is not saying that a believer's life will be easy. Paul is saying that one day we will all be made whole again in the presence of God, and no matter what may come, we must use all of it to bring us closer to God. No situation in life is hopeless and beyond God's ability to heal. With God, there is always hope! The days of Isaiah were difficult, as were many other moments in our spiritual history, and yet here we stand today as believers and followers of the same God! The Lord can truly work all things together for good. Trust in Him and His power!

## CONCLUSION

Praise be to God that His ways and thoughts are out of this world! In like manner, the Lord challenges us to live in a way that reflects His character and wisdom from above (Jas 3:16–18). Our lives tell a story about the God we serve to the world around us. We are a people molded and shaped by the extraordinary love of God, and our life should reflect that wonderful truth.

In addition, Isaiah 55 reminds us that even when the world makes us believe that all hope is gone, the Lord reminds us that His grace and mercy are also unlike anything we will experience in this world. May the encouraging words of Isaiah 55 be an encouragement to us all as we continue on our journey in the Lord! May the Lord bless you and keep you always!

## DISCUSSION QUESTIONS

1. God's thoughts and ways are out of this world! How do you stay connected to God's wisdom and love from above?
2. Isaiah 55:10–11 are two well known passages in Scripture. These verses speak to the certainty of God's proclamations and promises. They also speak to God's pattern of faithfulness. What does God's pattern of faithfulness look like in your life? How has He cared for you and provided for you?
3. Despite the abundance of evidence of God's providence and blessing in our lives, why do we still go through moments of anxiety and worry?
4. When we are shaped by the wisdom from above, our actions will show a clear difference with the world around us. However, Peter tells us that being an influencer for God will not be easy and may cause some to criticize us (1 Pet 4:3–4). What are some best practices to help keep you strong and on the right path?

# GOD'S ANOINTED

## Isaiah 61

### Jeremy Barrier

## FOCUS PASSAGE

Isaiah 61

1 The Spirit of the Lord God is upon me; because the Lord hath anointed me to preach good tidings unto the meek; he hath sent me to bind up the brokenhearted, to proclaim liberty to the captives, and the opening of the prison to them that are bound; 2 To proclaim the acceptable year of the Lord, and the day of vengeance of our God; to comfort all that mourn; 3 To appoint unto them that mourn in Zion, to give unto them beauty for ashes, the oil of joy for mourning, the garment of praise for the spirit of heaviness; that they might be called trees of righteousness, the planting of the Lord, that he might be glorified. 4 And they shall build the old wastes, they shall raise up

the former desolations, and they shall repair the waste cities, the desolations of many generations. 5 And strangers shall stand and feed your flocks, and the sons of the alien shall be your plowmen and your vinedressers. 6 But ye shall be named the Priests of the Lord: men shall call you the Ministers of our God: ye shall eat the riches of the Gentiles, and in their glory shall ye boast yourselves. 7 For your shame ye shall have double; and for confusion they shall rejoice in their portion: therefore in their land they shall possess the double: everlasting joy shall be unto them. 8 For I the Lord love judgment, I hate robbery for burnt offering; and I will direct their work in truth, and I will make an everlasting covenant with them. 9 And their seed shall be known among the Gentiles, and their offspring among the people: all that see them shall acknowledge them, that they are the seed which the Lord hath blessed. 10 I will greatly rejoice in the Lord, my soul shall be joyful in my God; for he hath clothed me with the garments of salvation, he hath covered me with the robe of righteousness, as a bridegroom decketh himself with ornaments, and as a bride adorneth herself with her jewels. 11 For as the earth bringeth forth her bud, and as the garden causeth the things that are sown in it to spring forth; so the Lord God will cause righteousness and praise to spring forth before all the nations. (KJV)

## ONE MAIN THING

God has sent his anointed one, the Messiah, to bring healing, freedom, righteousness, and redemption to his people. He will not forget to attend to the cries of those who are hurting. Knowing that God provides away for deliverance allows us to hold on to hope during difficult times.

## INTRODUCTION

One of the greatest empires that the world has ever seen was that of the Incan Empire. The remnants of this mighty people have inspired us today through such places as Machu Picchu, advanced irrigation systems, or even mystic legends and curiosities associated with elongated skulls presumably from their Inkan royalty. The awesomeness of this ancient empire is complemented as well by the greatness of its fall to the Spanish. The last of the royal monarchs of the Incan Empire to fall to the Spanish was that of Túpac Amaru, who was executed in September of 1572, and greatly mourned by the mountain people of the Andes. Roughly two hundred years later, the memory of Túpac Amaru was kindled in the beginnings of the Peruvian struggle for independence, when another leader arose, Túpac Amaru II. While his rebellion led to his violent death and the death of his family in the year 1781, his efforts did lead to the defeat of the Spanish by Perú nearly half a century later. The struggle for freedom, equality, justice, and fairness is sometimes hard to earn. The struggle for justice and freedom takes place in many cultures and in many settings. Such was the case for the Jews in Palestine 2000 years ago. When the young Jew by the name of Jesus arose before his synagogue in Nazareth to read from the Holy Scriptures, he too brought a message of longing for independence. His message came from the great prophet of old by the name of Isaiah. Jesus told his synagogue that he would be the one who had been "anointed by God." It would be Jesus who would bring release to the unjustly imprisoned. For those who were in debt to landlords, Jesus would usher in the "new year," the year that all debts in Israel would be forgiven. Jesus would bring hope to the hopeless and poor. Jesus would bring healing to those who were blind. Jesus would be the long expected king of Israel who would arise and heal the land. This story is told in Luke 4:14–29 for those who want to read it.

## GOING DEEPER

What is amazing is that the heart of Jesus's message comes from the reading of the Scriptures of Isaiah. Isaiah was a renowned and famous prophet of Israel, who had lived some 800 years before Jesus. However, by the time of Jesus's life, his writings were certainly one of the most important and popular writings by the Jewish people. His writings were a great source of inspiration.

In particular, the final section of the book in chapters 56–66 proclaimed a great redeeming message of deliverance by God. Isaiah called out the words of a God who would redeem and heal the nation of Israel. Isaiah brought a message of returning "anointed one", a King like no other king of old, who would heal and deliver the people. One passage that communicates this message so clearly is the one that Jesus read within his community that had gathered on the Sabbath. He was reading Isaiah 61. The message of Isaiah emphasizes that God will bring justice to the people of God through this anointed one. God loves justice (Isa 61:8; 11). God rejoices in seeing everyone treated with fairness. Ultimately, what Isaiah is calling for is the fairness, independence, and equality that all humans deserve. This is the message of Isaiah. Consequently, his was the core message of Jesus too. Jesus, the anointed one of God, who would bring justice and mercy to the world through his life. An amazing message indeed!

## APPLICATION

Sometimes we struggle under the weight of the world. We carry so many burdens. Sometimes we simply cannot make enough money to survive. We struggle with our families. We struggle in our marriages. We struggle with our children. We struggle with our work. We struggle with our health. We struggle in our spirit. Our soul cries out to be filled. We hurt. We long for more. We desire love. We desire affection. We desire to have meaning. So many difficulties and trials weigh us down. Then, we read the message of Isaiah 61. After reading Isaiah's message, he fills us with hope and justice.

## CONCLUSION

We realize that the anointed one will bring freedom from oppression, and God will deliver. Similarly, by way of comparison the Incan people desired redemption. The people of ancient Israel also cried to God for redemption in the sending of a deliverer. Even in the days of Jesus, the people gathered in the synagogues of Galilee and specifically in Nazareth, and they called out to God for healing. Through the message of Isaiah God says he will provide. This is a message of hope!

## DISCUSSION

1. What are some of the deeds and actions that the anointed one mentions doing for his people Israel?
2. When the anointed one says he will give "sight to the blind" or that he will "bind up the brokenhearted," how does this make you feel?
3. If you could think of a time when you felt

very low, was it difficult to read and believe a passage like Isaiah 61? What can you do to make it easier to hold on to hope and trust in God?

4. When Jesus read the words of Isaiah 61 before his hometown synagogue of Nazareth, and proclaimed that "This day is this Scripture fulfilled in your ears" (Luke 4:21; KJV), how does this make you feel about Jesus? How does it make you feel about your faith?

# Scripture Index

## Old Testament

### Genesis
| | |
|---|---|
| 1 | 17, 95 |
| 12:3 | 26 |
| 49:10 | 32 |

### Exodus
| | |
|---|---|
| 19:16–20 | 15 |
| 20:4–6 | 82 |
| 24:6–8 | 99 |
| 25:10–22 | 15 |
| 28:17 | 10 |
| 28:41 | 31 |
| 29:21 | 99 |
| 30:30 | 31 |
| 33:20 | 14 |
| 40:15 | 31 |

### Leviticus
| | |
|---|---|
| 4:3 | 31 |
| 4:5 | 31 |
| 4:16 | 31 |
| 6:15 | 31 |
| 8:11 | 99 |
| 14:7 | 99 |
| 16 | 17, 104 |
| 16:6 | 17 |
| 16:14–16 | 99 |
| 16:22 | 102 |

### Numbers
| | |
|---|---|
| 3:3 | 31 |
| 24:17 | 32 |
| 35:25 | 31 |

### Deuteronomy
| | |
|---|---|
| 4:5–6 | 109–110 |
| 4:7 | 110 |
| 10:14–15 | 110 |
| 32:43 | 26 |

### 1 Samuel
| | |
|---|---|
| 2:10 | 31 |
| 2:35 | 31 |
| 12:3 | 31 |
| 12:5 | 31 |
| 16 | 23 |
| 16:6 | 31 |
| 16:7 | 25 |

| | | | |
|---|---|---|---|
| 20:27 | 24 | 93:1 | 90 |
| 20:30–31 | 24 | 97:1 | 30, 90 |
| 22:7–13 | 24 | 117:1 | 26 |
| 24:7 | 31 | 132 | 15 |
| 24:11 | 31 | **Isaiah** | |
| 26:9 | 31 | 1 | xv |
| 29:11 | 31 | 1–5 | 16 |
| 26:16 | 31 | 1–39 | xiii |
| 26:23 | 31 | 1:1 | xi, xiii |
| **2 Samuel** | | 1:2 | xvi |
| 1:14 | 31 | 1:2–3 | xvi, 80 |
| 1:16 | 31 | 1:3 | xvi |
| 1:21 | 31 | 1:18 | 99 |
| 7:12–13 | 32 | 2 | 2 |
| 7:12–16 | 24 | 2–4 | 2 |
| 19:22 | 31 | 2–12 | xiv–xv |
| 22:51 | 31 | 2:1 | xiii–xiv |
| 23:1 | 31 | 2:1–5 | 3 |
| **1 Kings** | | 2:1–22 | 3 |
| 3 | 25 | 2:2 | 3 |
| 18:20–40 | 36 | 2:2–4 | 1 |
| **2 Kings** | | 2:2–5 | 1, 3, 10 |
| 24–25 | xii | 2:2–5:30 | 10 |
| | | 2:3 | 3–4, 9–10 |
| **2 Chronicles** | | | |
| 9:17 | 15 | 2:5 | 4, 6, 11 |
| 26:5 | 14 | 2:6–9 | 6 |
| 28:2 | 15 | 2:6–22 | 3, 6, 10 |
| **Ezra** | | 2:8–9 | 10 |
| 1:1–4 | xiii | 2:10–12 | 6 |
| **Job** | | 2:12 | 10 |
| 1–2 | 17 | 2:13–17 | 7 |
| 38–41 | 81 | 2:17 | 11 |
| **Psalms** | | 2:21–22 | 11 |
| 18:49 | 26 | 4:2–6 | 10 |
| 23:6 | 10 | 6 | xii, 13, 85 |

| | | | |
|---|---|---|---|
| 6:1 | 12, 15 | 25:6–8 | 34–36, 39 |
| 6:1–13 | 12 | 25:7 | 36 |
| 6:3 | 15, 19 | 25:8 | 37, 45 |
| 6:4 | 15 | 25:9–12 | 35, 37 |
| 6:8 | 17, 92 | 25:10 | 36–37 |
| 6:9 | 13 | 26 | 43, 45 |
| 7 | xiv | 26:1–6 | 43–44 |
| 7:1–2 | 24 | 26:3 | 47 |
| 7:14 | 20, 62 | 28 | 52, 54, 56–58 |
| 9:6–7 | 20, 62 | | |
| 11 | 23, 29, 32 | 28–30 | 34 |
| 11:1–5 | 62 | 28–35 | xv |
| 11:1–10 | 20, 30 | 28:1–13 | 55 |
| 11:2 | 24 | 28:5 | 55 |
| 11:3 | 25 | 28:5–6 | 54–55 |
| 11:4 | 25 | 28:7 | 59 |
| 11:6–9 | 25–26, 30 | 28:14 | 59 |
| 11:10 | 26 | 28:14–19 | 55 |
| 13–14 | xiv | 28:16 | 60 |
| 13–23 | xiv–xv | 32 | 61, 67 |
| 13–24 | 44 | 32:1 | 15 |
| 13–25 | 34 | 32:1–2 | 61 |
| 13:1 | xiv | 32:1–8 | 32 |
| 14:23 | xiv | 32:5 | 67 |
| 14:24–27 | xiv | 32:6 | 67 |
| 14:29–32 | xiv | 32:7 | 67 |
| 15–16 | xiv | 34 | 72 |
| 24 | 44 | 34:1–2 | 72 |
| 24–27 | xv | 34:7 | 72 |
| 24:23 | 15, 36 | 34:13–14 | 72 |
| 25 | 34–35, 37–38 | 35 | 72, 74, 77 |
| | | 35:2 | 74 |
| 25–27 | 35 | 35:4 | 72, 74 |
| 25:1–5 | 35 | 35:5–6 | 72 |
| 25:3–4 | 44 | 35:8–10 | 69, 76–77 |
| 25:6 | 36 | 36–37 | xii |

| | |
|---|---|
| 36–39 | xiv–xv |
| 37:16 | 18 |
| 39 | xiv |
| 39:5–8 | 80 |
| 40 | 79–81, 83–85 |
| 40–48 | xii |
| 40–66 | xiii |
| 40:1–2 | 84 |
| 40:3–5 | 84 |
| 40:3–8 | 81 |
| 40:6 | 84 |
| 40:6–7 | 81 |
| 40:6–30 | 81 |
| 40:8 | 81 |
| 40:10 | 81 |
| 40:12–26 | 18 |
| 40:15 | 82 |
| 40:19–20 | 82 |
| 40:22 | 82 |
| 40:24 | 82 |
| 40:28 | 82 |
| 40:28–31 | 79 |
| 40:29 | 83 |
| 40:30 | 83 |
| 40:31 | 81, 83 |
| 40:37–38 | 82 |
| 44:28 | xiii |
| 45:1 | xiii |
| 48:20 | xii |
| 49:4 | 98 |
| 50:2 | 98 |
| 51:9 | 99 |
| 51:18 | 98 |
| 52 | 92 |
| 52:1 | 93 |
| 52:1–2 | 92 |
| 52:6 | 92 |
| 52:7 | 89–91 |
| 52:7–10 | 87, 91 |
| 52:8–9b | 91 |
| 52:9c–10 | 91 |
| 52:10 | 99 |
| 52:10–53:12 | 97 |
| 52:13–15 | 99 |
| 52:13–53:1 | 99 |
| 52:14 | 99 |
| 52:15 | 99 |
| 53 | 97–99, 102–104 |
| 53:1 | 92, 99, 104 |
| 53:2 | 100 |
| 53:2–3 | 100 |
| 53:3 | 100 |
| 53:4 | 101, 104 |
| 53:4–6 | 101 |
| 53:4–9 | 100 |
| 53:5 | 99, 101 |
| 53:6 | 101–102 |
| 53:7 | 101 |
| 53:7–8 | 98 |
| 53:10 | 101 |
| 53:11 | 103 |
| 54:9 | 108 |
| 55 | 108, 113 |
| 55:2 | 111 |
| 55:3 | 110 |
| 55:6–7 | 108, 111 |
| 55:8–9 | 107–109 |
| 55:10–11 | 111, 114 |
| 56–66 | 119 |
| 57:15 | 18 |

| | | | |
|---|---|---|---|
| 58:12 | 90 | 9:11 | 32 |
| 61 | 115, 119–121 | 9:11–12 | 32 |
| 61:1–11 | 115–116 | **Micah** | |
| 61:8 | 119 | 5:1–5 | 32 |
| 61:11 | 119 | **Zechariah** | |
| 65:17 | xiii, 25 | 9:1–10 | 32 |
| 65:17–20 | 57 | | |
| 65:25 | 25 | | |
| 66:24 | 80 | **New Testament** | |
| **Jeremiah** | | **Matthew** | |
| 7 | 56 | 1:1 | 27 |
| 23:5–8 | 32 | 7:28–29 | 100 |
| 25 | xii | 8:17 | 104 |
| 30:9 | 32 | 12:42 | 25 |
| 32:38 | 11 | 13:35 | 38 |
| 33:14–26 | 32 | 16:13–20 | 32 |
| 46–51 | xiv | 16:21 | 27 |
| **Ezekiel** | | 18:15–20 | 50 |
| 17:22–24 | 32 | 21:42 | 60 |
| 25–32 | xiv | 25:31–46 | 55 |
| 34:23–24 | 23, 32 | 28:18 | 28 |
| 37:15–28 | 32 | 28:18–20 | 91, 93, 110 |
| 37:24–25 | 23 | **Mark** | |
| **Daniel** | | 1:1–2 | xxii |
| 2 | 2 | 1:2 | ix |
| 2:44 | 2, 9 | 1:15 | 28 |
| 7:13–14 | 32 | 8:27–30 | 32 |
| 9:24–27 | 22 | 8:29 | 27 |
| **Hosea** | | 8:31 | 27 |
| 3:5 | 32 | 10:35–45 | 100 |
| 11:1–4 | 111 | 12:10 | 60 |
| **Joel** | | 16:15 | 91 |
| 2 | 2 | **Luke** | |
| 2:28–32 | 2, 9 | 2:14 | 26 |
| 3:10 | 10 | 2:46–47 | 100 |
| **Amos** | | 4:14–29 | 118 |

| | | | |
|---|---|---|---|
| 4:21 | 121 | 18:8 | 28 |
| 5:8 | 16 | **Romans** | |
| 9:18–20 | 32 | 1 | 64 |
| 9:22 | 27 | 1:16–17 | 62–63 |
| 11:31 | 25 | 1:17 | 63 |
| 15:1–2 | 100 | 1:18 | 63–64 |
| 15:11–32 | 95 | 3:5 | 65 |
| 16:14 | 100 | 3:9 | 66 |
| 20:17 | 60 | 3:21 | 66 |
| 24:47 | 10 | 3:22 | 66 |
| **John** | | 5:1 | 47 |
| 1:11 | 100 | 6:7 | 92 |
| 1:12 | 29 | 8:28 | 112 |
| 1:14 | 54, 74 | 9:33 | 60 |
| 1:29 | 101 | 10:9 | 28 |
| 1:45–46 | 100 | 10:11 | 60 |
| 12:37–43 | 14 | 10:14–15 | 91 |
| 12:48 | 100, 103–104 | 10:15 | 91 |
| 14:1–3 | 84 | 10:16 | 92, 100, 103–104 |
| 18:11 | 101 | 11:22 | 10 |
| **Acts** | | 15:4 | 83 |
| 1:6 | 11 | 15:7–13 | 26 |
| 1:8 | 91 | 15:8–9 | 26 |
| 2 | 5, 9 | 16:25–26 | 38 |
| 2:1–47 | 9 | **1 Corinthians** | |
| 2:5 | 10 | 3:11 | 56 |
| 2:14–21 | 2 | 10:11 | 83 |
| 2:36 | 28 | 15:26 | 37 |
| 4:11 | 60 | **2 Corinthians** | |
| 8:31 | 98 | 1:3 | 83 |
| 8:31–35 | 98 | 5:21 | 101–102 |
| 8:34 | 98 | 12:9 | 88 |
| 8:35–38 | 98 | **Galatians** | |
| 10:35 | 10 | 3:8 | 26 |
| 17:3 | 28 | 3:15–16 | 26 |
| 18:5 | 28 | | |

| | | | |
|---|---|---|---|
| 3:27 | 92 | 1 John | |
| 5:16 | 92 | 1:7 | 10, 103 |
| **Ephesians** | | 2:1–2 | 103 |
| 1:4 | 38 | 2:5–6 | 103 |
| 2:17 | 50 | **Revelation** | |
| 4:1–3 | 49 | 1:9 | 9 |
| 5:14 | 92 | 2:10 | 11 |
| 6:10–11 | 93 | 4:8 | 16 |
| 6:13–20 | 93 | 19:9 | 39 |
| **Philippians** | | 20:7–15 | 37 |
| 2:4 | 49 | 21:1–4 | 84 |
| 2:5 | 103 | 21:4 | 36 |
| 2:6–11 | 104 | | |
| 2:11 | 28 | | |
| 4:7 | 45 | | |
| **Colossians** | | | |
| 1:13 | 9 | | |
| 2:6–7 | 103 | | |
| 3:15 | 47–48 | | |
| **1 Thessalonians** | | | |
| 2:12 | 9 | | |
| 4:13–18 | 84 | | |
| **2 Timothy** | | | |
| 1:9 | 38 | | |
| **Hebrews** | | | |
| 11 | 13 | | |
| 11:37 | 13 | | |
| 11:37–38 | 13 | | |
| 12:2–3 | 101 | | |
| **James** | | | |
| 3:16–18 | 113 | | |
| **1 Peter** | | | |
| 3:16 | xv | | |
| 4:3–4 | 114 | | |
| **2 Peter** | | | |
| 3:18 | 49 | | |

Ancient Literature

**Psalms of Solomon**

17:21–32    32

**1 Enoch**

48:10–49:4    32

**Babylonian Talmud Tractate,** *Sanhedrin*

93b    32

# CONTRIBUTORS

**Bill Bagents** (DMin Amridge University) is Professor of Ministry, Counseling and Biblical Studies at Heritage Christian University, Florence, Alabama, USA.

**Jeremy Barrier** (PhD Brite Divinity School, Texas Christian University) is Professor of Biblical Literature at Heritage Christian University, Florence, Alabama, USA.

**Ismael Berlanga** (DMin Lincoln Christian University) has worked with congregations in Central Texas, most recently as the Minister at the Second and Wallace Church of Christ in San Saba, Texas.

**W. Kirk Brothers** (PhD Southern Baptist Theological Seminary) is President of Heritage Christian University, Florence, Alabama, USA.

**Will Dilbeck** (PhD Hebrew Union College) is an instructor in biblical studies at Florida College, Temple Terrace, Florida, USA.

**Ed Gallagher** (PhD Hebrew Union College is Professor of Christian Scripture at Heritage Christian University, Florence, Alabama, USA.

**Justin Guin** (MDiv Freed-Hardeman University is Adjunct Instructor at Heritage Christian University, Florence, Alabama, USA.

**Michael Jackson** (EdD Union University is Vice President of Academic Affairs and Associate Professor of Education and New Testament at Heritage Christian University, Florence, Alabama, USA.

**Todd Johnson** (MMin Heritage Christian University serves as Executive Director for the Tennessee Children's Home - West Campus in Pinson, Tennessee, USA.

**C. Wayne Kilpatrick** (MAR Harding School of Theology is Emeritus Professor of Church History at Heritage Christian University, Florence, Alabama, USA.

**Tim Martin** (Pursuing: PhD in New Testament Studies Amridge University) is the Education Minister for the Mt. Juliet Church of Christ, Mt. Juliet, Tennessee, USA.

**Keith Stanglin** (PhD is Professor of Theology at Heritage Christian University, Florence, Alabama, USA.

**Thomas Tidwell** (MA Heritage Christian University) is an elder and preacher at the South Cobb church of Christ, and the Director of the Marietta Campus of Georgia School of Preaching and Biblical Studies in Marietta, Georgia, USA.

# CREDITS

Select Scripture quotations are taken from the NEW AMERICAN STANDARD BIBLE®, copyright© 1960, 1962, 1963, 1968, 1971, 1972, 1973, 1975, 1977, 1995 by The Lockman Foundation. Used by permission.

Select Scripture quotations are taken from the NEW KING JAMES VERSION®. Copyright© 1982 by Thomas Nelson, Inc. Used by permission. All rights reserved.

Select Scripture quotations are taken from the NEW REVISED STANDARD VERSION BIBLE, copyright © 1989 National Council of the Churches of Christ in the United States of America. Used by permission. All rights reserved worldwide.

Select Scriptures quotations are taken from the Holy Bible, New International Version®, NIV®. Copyright © 1973, 1978, 1984, 2011 by Biblica, Inc.™ Used by permission of Zondervan. All rights reserved worldwide. www.zondervan.com The "NIV" and "New International Version" are trademarks registered in the

United States Patent and Trademark Office by Biblica, Inc.®

Scripture quotations marked HCSB are been taken from the Holman Christian Standard Bible®, Copyright © 1999, 2000, 2002, 2003 by Holman Bible Publishers. Used by permission. Holman Christian Standard Bible®, Holman CSB®, and HCSB® are federally registered trademarks of Holman Bible Publishers.

Scripture quotations from The Authorized (King James) Version. Rights in the Authorized Version in the United Kingdom are vested in the Crown. Reproduced by permission of the Crown's patentee, Cambridge University Press.

Scripture quotations are from the ESV® Bible (The Holy Bible, English Standard Version®), copyright © 2001 by Crossway, a publishing ministry of Good News Publishers. Used by permission. All rights reserved

Scripture quotations taken from the (NASB®) New American Standard Bible®, Copyright © 1960, 1971, 1977, 1995 by The Lockman Foundation. Used by permission. All rights reserved. www.lockman.org"

# BEREAN STUDY SERIES TITLES

*For the Glory of God: Christ and the Church in Ephesians* (2021)

*Cloud of Witnesses: Ancient Stories of Faith* (2020)

*Visions of Grace* (2019)

*Instructions for Living: The Ten Commandments* (2018)

*Clothed in Christ: A How-to Guide* (2017)

*What Does Real Christianity Look Like? A Study of the Parables* (2016)

*The Ekklesia of Christ: Becoming the People of God* (2015)

## COMING IN 2023

The theme for the 2023 Berean Study Series is:
*Led by God's Spirit: A Practical Study of Galatians 5:16–26*

www.ingramcontent.com/pod-product-compliance
Lightning Source LLC
Chambersburg PA
CBHW021426070526
44577CB00001B/77

To see full catalog of Heritage Christian University
Press and its imprint Cypress Publications, visit
www.hcu.edu/publications